THE INNS AND AI
OF
CHIPPING CAI... ...
AND
BROAD CAMPDEN

A Pub Trail
round Chipping Campden and Broad Campden
with a historical account of the pubs and anecdotes from their past

Compiled for CADHAS by **Celia Jones**

in a team research project with **Hilary Sinclair** and **Dorothy Brook**

Campden & District Historical & Archæological Society

ISBN 0-9511434-5-X

Printed in England by The Vale Press Ltd

A project such as this has no end and this booklet is by no means definitive. CADHAS would be very pleased to hear from anyone who has any further information, or any corrections to what is here.

For this booklet documents and maps in Record Offices and libraries, Victuallers' Recognizances, Petty Sessions Records, trade directories, the Post Office directory, the census, the History Society's archives, material at the Guild of Handicraft Trust, local newspapers, and books were all consulted. Many local people supplied information and stories. Photographs are from the CADHAS archive, the Guild of Handicraft Trust, Hilary Sinclair, Allan Warmington and Clive Bennett.

Compiled for CADHAS by **Celia Jones**

in a team research project with **Hilary Sinclair** and **Dorothy Brook**

and pleasant hours researching beer in The Volunteer

ACKNOWLEDGEMENTS

A major source for this document is Peter Gordon's scholarly and readable account of the Title Deeds of houses in Chipping Campden, from which all mention of deeds has been taken. He generously gave access to his work in progress. Many anecdotes and much information came from Fred Coldicott, given with characteristic humour and wit. Diana Harding's helpful provision of ideas and first-hand knowledge has been greatly valued. Allan Warmington gave much assistance, supplied anecdotes and kindly checked facts. Craig Fees, whose doctoral thesis on Chipping Campden (1988) contains a wealth of knowledge about the town, generously lent his research notes. Frank Johnson helped with Guild of Handicraft Trust material. Rosemary Turner supplied fruitful ideas and quotations, and helped with the CADHAS archive. Jill Wilson provided starting points and information from her wide knowledge of Campden's history. Neville New's lively writing evoked the past vividly. Tim Jones gave research help. And of course Carol Jackson deserves thanks for always being ready with material, suggestions and encouragement.

Many people willingly gave their time, knowledge (and often refreshments), and thanks are due to all of them, including: Graeme Black, Geoffrey Douglass, Pam and David Atkinson, Sandra Potter, Jean Ellis, Christine Ackerman, Molly Potter, Keith Moule, Freda Hopkins, Barbara Rawcliffe, Sue Durrant, Alex Pennycock, Nancy Smith, Dorothy Stanley, Jean Jones, Neville Date and Michael Drew.

Last and by no means least gratitude has been earned by Bob Jones, who typed, discussed, revised, and typed again.

THE INNS AND ALEHOUSES OF

CHIPPING CAMPDEN AND BROAD CAMPDEN

There is nothing which has yet been contrived
by man, by which so much happiness is
produced as by a good tavern or inn.
Samuel Johnson, 1776

CERTAINLY the people of Campden, from earliest times to the present
day, would agree with Dr Johnson. Inns have always been important in
Campden's history. During the Second World War the Home Guard's
choice of assembly points showed their feeling for the most significant
places in the town: in the first part of the day they assembled at
    10 a.m. at The Eight Bells,
    11 a.m. at The Lygon Arms,
    12 noon at The Noel Arms,
    1 p.m. at The Red Lion,
    2 p.m. at The Volunteer;
and in the evening, at the same venues in the reverse order. One wonders
how they ever managed to defend the realm.

Inns, Taverns, Alehouses, Public Houses and Hotels

In pre-industrial England there were three kinds of place for drinking in: the inn, the tavern and the alehouse. But people were vague about definitions, and in country areas particularly the distinctions between the different kinds of establishment were ofter blurred. A further complication was the different names given to the alehouse in the Tudor and Stuart period - tippling houses, boozing kens, and more locally, as in Campden, beerhouses. As late as 1889, when John Lane, who had kept The Live and Let Live, bought Saxton House (for £230), he was referred to as a Beerhouse Keeper.

At the end of the seventeenth century the term alehouse slowly gave way to that of public house, but public house might also include taverns and inns. Also the alehouses started to take on the grander name of the inn.

Nevertheless it is possible to distinguish generally between inns, usually large fashionable establishments offering wine, ale and beer, food and lodgings to prosperous travellers; taverns, selling wine to the better-off but without the accommodation of inns; and alehouses, smaller premises selling ale or beer and sometimes providing basic food and accommodation for the ordinary people. The same categories were recognised in law from the sixteenth century in licensing and the legal obligations of landlords.

The Noel Arms

In medieval times, and increasingly so by Tudor times, the inn had great importance. A statute of Richard II in 1393 made it compulsory for English inns to display a sign. The inn was a commercial and trading centre where bargains could be struck and goods stored in warehouses; often it produced its own tokens which were used as currency. Inns were often used as wool marts. They were important as staging-posts for transport and communication. They provided coach services for the well-to-do, and from the seventeenth century innkeepers acted as provincial postmasters for the expanding Post Office. Auctions of property and land usually took place in inns. They were also social centres where feasts, balls, debates, gambling, cock-fighting (at The Lygon Arms, then called The Hare And Hounds, and The Green Dragon in Campden), trade associations, election gatherings and all manner of entertainment happened. Particularly in the seventeenth century plays would be acted, and in the nineteenth century the Noel Arms Assembly Room was used for plays and opera. Interestingly enough even in the 1930s and after the war the Osiris Players, a travelling troupe of women players, performed Shakespeare at The Noel Arms, in the yard.

During the last war many pubs and their buildings were used as billets for soldiers.

At the other end of the scale the alehouse catered for the needs of small farmers, artisans and labourers. The premises were small, often a front room or parlour, and frequently a widow would run the business, brewing her own ale and making a living in one of the few ways open to her. Alehouses would come and go, unfortunately usually without trace, but no doubt Campden was well supplied. In the early twentieth century and even after the second world war the successors of the alehouses, the public houses, often ran "pub clubs", which were a kind of mutual insurance before the Welfare State. Nearly every pub in Campden had its club. The Lygon's club, for example, organised trips to the sea-side for its members.

Somewhere between the inn and the alehouse the tavern bridged the

"K" Company, 2nd V. B. Glo'ster Regiment.

A
VOLUNTEER
BALL
Under the Patronage of
THE VISCOUNT and VISCOUNTESS LIFFORD
THE REV. CANON BOURNE, C.C., J.P.
MR. and MRS. BRUCE
CAPTAIN and MRS. H. M. SPENCER
LIEUT. and MRS. C. MORRIS,
&c., &c.
WILL BE HELD AT THE
ASSEMBLY ROOMS, NOEL ARMS,
CAMPDEN,
On Monday, March 4th, 1889,
When the pleasure of the company of

----

is requested.

Ladies 3s. Gentlemen 4s.
(Light Refreshments included.)

gap.

At the end of the eighteenth century French fashions were popular. Innkeepers refurbished their houses, making them elegant and private, and called them hotels. This trend reached the countryside very much later. The Lygon Arms was called a "commercial inn" in 1904 when Annie Jeffrey was licensee; by John Skey's time, in 1917, it was known as The Lygon Arms Hotel.

Until recently innkeepers and beerhouse keepers usually had another occupation, and often several activities would go on in the same building.

There were always many licensed houses in Campden. In 1755, for example, the Justices of the Peace's record of Victuallers' Recognizances shows 25 licensed victuallers in the town, who were required to "keep good order and suffer no disorder to be committed or unlawful games used in their said houses yards gardens or backsides thereunto belonging during the continuance of their respective licences." In 1891 the Petty Sessions records show 38 licensed houses; in 1903 there were 36. This was not unusual: Winchcombe had 39. For a town of under two thousand inhabitants this was, however, a generous allocation - perhaps there were some who considered it too generous. The Petty Sessions records reveal quite a few prosecutions for drunkenness and disorderliness, fighting, drunk in charge of a horse and cart. Slap Blakeman, a local character often the worse for tippling, was once so drunk that his friends dismantled his cart, took it into the house where they were and put it back together again so that he could

Slap Blakeman

not get into it and let his horse take him home. In 1893 a man named Cherry was convicted of being drunk. The arresting officer testified: "...he was drunk and playing the concertina - he played in tune.."

At the beginning of the twentieth century social trends against drinking were certainly evident. During the first war alcohol was fairly scarce and the men were away, but when the war ended and the men returned there was a move to close six of the existing pubs. These were The Swan, The George and Dragon, The Angel in Broad Campden, The

Live and Let Live, The Rose and Crown, and The Plough. They all catered for labouring folk. Appeals were heard but sadly all six lost their licences.

Malting and Brewing

Malt was made from barley, which was selected and prepared for the *mash-tun* by steeping it in water, renewing the water every 24 hours. After three or four days the water was drained off and the barley was cast onto the malting floor to germinate. As soon as growth began the barley was thinned out. In well regulated malt-barns good provision was made for fresh air, which was essential to regular growth. Water was sprinkled to encourage growth. When ready the malt was removed to the drying area, with wire cloth floors, a ventilator on top, and an open fire underneath. When dried the malt was crushed into *grist*, then fed into the mash-tun along with hot water making a consistency like porridge. As soon as the mash was finished the tun was covered up while fermentation took place. Then taps at the bottom of the mash-tun were opened to allow the extract to drain off through the perforated false bottom. A brewing extract or *wort* was produced in this way.

Ale was brewed from malt infused in water with the addition of some basic spices (but not hops), and was a heavy, thick drink which had to be consumed quickly before it deteriorated. It was fairly easy to produce. There was a custom of hanging a bush outside the house when the ale was ready.

Beer is an infusion of malted barley which has been boiled with hops and afterwards undergone fermentation. The hops, of which the female flower was used, purified and preserved the wort and gave it a characteristic aroma. Brewing beer was more complicated than brewing ale.

Beer brewing had arrived from the continent in the fifteenth century and gradually spread, until by the early seventeenth century ale was increasingly replaced by beer. This meant that the small landlord found it more difficult to do his own brewing. At the beginning of the seventeenth century there were a number of "common brewers" who would sell their beer locally to small establishments and some urban-based larger full-time brewers. After 1720 several of these large brewers cornered the market and small-scale brewing declined. Later in the eighteenth century the large brewers "tied" many public houses to their breweries. The beer act of 1830 relaxed the licensing laws and allowed publicans to be freer of the large breweries, but by the end of the nineteenth and throughout the twentieth century breweries were themselves buying pubs; for example in 1898 The Plough was sold to Hunt, Edmund & Co. of Banbury.

In the 1980s a monopolies commission attempted to restrict the monopolies of the large breweries who were forced to sell many pubs. Tenants were obliged to go and many of the pubs became private houses. A more recent development is that a company that is not a brewery owns a string of pubs, putting in managers to run them. Such are the shifting patterns of private and large-scale ownership.

Meanwhile, as ale was superseded by beer, the term *ale* quickly developed another meaning (true tipplers would never wish to waste "ale") and by 1700 it was used to describe light, high-quality beer.

There were several malthouses in Chipping Campden: there was one at Elm Tree House, which C.R.Ashbee[1] bought in 1902. He converted the malthouse for use as a lecture room and teaching space for the Guild of Handicraft.

There was a malthouse at Dover's House where F.L.Griggs[2] was tenant from 1906-1930. In 1907 Alec Miller, the sculptor, used the malthouse here, having escaped from Braithwaite House, the boarding-house for the single men in the Guild, where he presumably had little space. Dover's House malthouse was known as The Studio and was adapted by Ashbee into a dwelling as well as a workspace. Alec Miller moved into the malthouse in 1908 and lived there with his wife from their marriage in 1909 to 1924.

There was also a malthouse at Darby's House, and another next to the Seymour House Hotel.

In Broad Campden, according to J. P. Nelson, in his book on Broad Campden, there was a malthouse together with cottages. The last people to malt there were Mr and Mrs John Tomes. This long malthouse was converted by a young member of the Noel family[3] in 1905, the first malthouse to be converted for residential use. It is now a country guest house.

There were also many brewhouses, serving private individuals and public houses. The Hook Norton Brewery can trace its origins back to 1849 when a young man, John Harris, moved into Hook Norton and set up business as a maltster. He soon started brewing himself and in 1872 built a small three-storey brewery. In 1896 a six-storey brewery was built which is still in use today along with much of the original brewing equipment. Hook Norton is one of only forty surviving independent family-run breweries.

Large country houses also had their own brewhouses, the produce of which was used by the family and as part wages for those who worked on the estate, but was not for general sale. At Charlecote Park, near Stratford, there is a large well preserved brewhouse where the implements can be seen and the processes are described. The house produced its own beer for a long time. When Spencer Lucy married in 1848 a dinner was given for the tenants at which four hundred gallons of old ale, brewed at Charlecote, were drunk.

Stanway House, an Elizabethan house near Broadway, also has a brewhouse. It was used continuously until the first world war. At this time a "brewing woman" used to turn up each autumn on a bicycle to brew the year's barley crop. The brewhouse then lay idle until 1993 when brewer Alex Pennycock leased the old brewery from Lord Neidpath, the owner of Stanway House. In the brewhouse are two coppers built over log fires, possibly the only log-fired coppers in the country. The open cooler is still there, although only used for storage now; the rest of the equipment is newly installed. By tradition brewing was considered part of the housework, hence the term "brewster", a female brewer. The brewery now supplies pubs in the Cotswold area - including The Volunteer in Chipping Campden and The Dormy House Hotel between Campden and Broadway - with three beers: Stanny Bitter, at 4.5% a well balanced "bitter" beer; Lords-a-Leaping, at 4.5% a dark full-bodied beer with a strong crystal malt character; and Old Eccentric, at 5.5% a slightly bitter full-flavoured dark beer.

Lid Holes, also known as the Jug and Bottle

Mr Fred Coldicott, whose family have lived in Campden for a long time and whose *Memories of an Old Campdonian* contains a wealth of stories about the town, remembers that most pubs had lid holes, or hatches, where drink could be bought for consumption off the premises. They served as a compromise between being inside and outside the pub. The name "The Jug And Bottle" was often etched into the glass at the hatch. A lot of women, in their long skirts and jackets, would stop at the lid holes and enjoy a drink or two rather than going right into the pub, a stronghold of the men. One of these characters was Sal Botheridge, who would move from lid hole to lid hole. In *Shepherds' Country*, H. J. Massingham tells the story of Polly Waine, who lived in the Almshouses between The Eight Bells and St James's church. She would visit the church, but more often The Eight Bells, where she would buy a pint of porter at the lid hole. One evening, returning home, she met the vicar. The wind blew her cloak back and he saw what she was carrying. He enquired if she had any for him; but she said "No". "No! and for why?" asked the vicar. She replied, "Cos I'm too fond of it myself."

Polly Waine

At the beginning of the last war Mr. Allan Warmington, whose family also go back a long way in Campden, remembers delivering fire watch rotas and handing one in at The Red Lion through the lid hole.

The lid holes were still in use after the second world war, serving as simple off-licences.

THE KETTLE, Leysbourne   1.

The building dates from around 1640. It has two dormer windows, two mullioned windows and two bay windows. A cobbled side passage containing an old well and a pump in working order leads to the courtyard and garden. The huge kettle hanging outside, suspended on high, is a landmark. In front of the house is the curved green of Leysbourne, said to date from the times when there was a blacksmith working at the property; horses would be shod, then with their carts led round to turn back onto the street into town, so forming the curve. Timber framing can be seen in the passageway wall and there are beamed ceilings and flagged floors.

The Kettle is one of the oldest continuous business properties in the country. Originally it is said to have been a coaching-house.

The census of 1871 shows Thomas Moss, Public House Brewer, living here. Beer was probably brewed on the premises in the barn at the back of the house, now incorporated into the living accommodation. The garden and passageway slope down to the street and it would have been convenient to roll the barrels down to the front of the building. The census of 1881 lists James Haines, brazier, brewer and rate collector, as the householder. James "Tinker" Haines, who repaired kettles and pans, was the one who hung the huge kettle outside his shop as a sign of his trade. His daughter, Martha Dunn, told Norman Jewson[4] that her father had clung to old customs long after they had died out elsewhere, and

The Kettle

when she was a child the family still used pewter plates, cleaning them with elder twigs. The Kettle was also an off-licence. At the turn of the century it was owned by the Hook Norton brewery selling stouts and ales "off". In what is now the shop an iron bar remains fastened to a beam: barrels would have been hung here and beer served from their wooden taps.

Grocers' shops would often have off-licences for selling beer, wine and spirits; for example, in 1903 Wixey's shop at the corner of Church Street was granted a licence at the Petty Sessions. Mr Fred Coldicott's uncle took on the off-licence at the Kettle in 1912. He was also a greengrocer. People would drink sitting outside on the green in Leysbourne, or, as an old photograph shows, leaning against the front wall of the shop in the sun. The shop continued after the first war. Mr Nevill New, who lived in Campden until 1929, recalls that The Kettle "had some sort of licence at some time. I remember it as a greengrocer's shop run by Mrs Robert Coldicott. Her husband was among other things

9

an expert exterminator of rats and other vermin. Mrs Coldicott was a great charmer but we always thought she was a bit scatter-brained to run a business. However, she did carry it on for many years."

The greengrocer's shop was still there in the fifties when it was run by Mrs Agnes Allard and then it became a grocer's run by Mr Ray Crump. Later Mrs Muriel Tudor Jones ran a pottery here, and then Frank and Jane Kennedy had an antique pine shop.

THE EIGHT BELLS, Church Street   2.

The Eight Bells is very quaint, with its small height and immense roof and gables. Part of the building dates back to the fourteenth century; part is seventeenth century, and it was possibly originally two houses. It is said to have been an inn in the fifteenth century for masons working on St James's church tower, during which time the bells were stored in the yard. (Most of the existing parish church bells, an octave, belong to the seventeenth century.)

But there is a puzzle here, because there was another inn called The Old Eight Bells, where Leasebourne House and the Convent are now. Perhaps the name passed to the present Eight Bells after The Old Eight Bells ceased to be an inn.

The Eight Bells was always said to be the bellringers' pub, and for a time until the 1980s the sign depicted the peal of bells. The sign that is there in 1998 shows single-stick fighting on Dover's Hill, and is taken from an old picture in the British Museum.

In 1637 William Sellers, a cooper, owned the premises. In the eighteenth century Peter Stanley occupied the property. In the Campden Ratebook for 1821 there is an entry for "The Eight Bells Inn & malthouse & garden value £6 rates 3s." Sarah Hands is named as the owner occupier. In 1858 Slater's Directory lists Richard Andrews as landlord. The 1871 census shows George Ireson as innkeeper, and Kelly's Directory of Gloucestershire of 1894 lists George Freeman, Innkeeper.

In 1898 the Compton Steam Brewery at Little Compton was put up for auction. The sale included tied houses, two of which were in Campden: The Volunteer and The Old Eight Bells (interestingly enough referred to as "Old"). The latter contained

"A stone and slate-roof gabled House with Gate and stone-paved Cartway in centre. Containing Tap Room, Bar, Kitchen, Sitting Room, Scullery, Cellar and Parlour, and four Bed Rooms. Yard with upland cellar, Stable and Loft and a brick, slated and tiled Building behind containing a spacious Club or Ball Room above and Skittle Alley below, standing stable and store House, Garden, Pig-sty, W.C. etc.

ALSO

A cottage adjoining under similar roof and of similar construction. The whole let to Mr G. Freeman, at £17 per annum. Leasehold for the residue of a term of 3,000 years from 25th March 1650 at a rent of 10s., and a couple of Hens."

In 1910 Kelly's Directory named Mrs Millicent Gladwin as householder. After her husband died she married Edwin Ladbrook, Pork Butcher. She taught cooking at the Grammar School, and was said to make the best faggots. During the war Mr and Mrs Tom Harris were the landlords. Mr Nevill New has early recollections of early mornings around 1914 when from his nursery window at Ivy House he watched many customers entering and leaving The Eight Bells on their way to work. Before the Defence of the Realm Act was passed later in the 1914-18 war and introduced new licensing procedures the pubs opened around 5.30 each morning.

From 1921 to 1953 Mr James Sadler and then his son Sam ran the pub. James Sadler, besides being landlord, also farmed and was responsible for introducing sprouts, now such an important crop, to the area. His son Sam was verger and sexton at St. James's Church. He rang the curfew every night at 8 o'clock, Saturdays at 7, on the church bells, and ended with the treble bell tolling the day of the month. The curfew had been rung for a long time and it carried on until the war. He also wound the clock and the chimes, letting a trap door down after 9 o'clock so there would be no chimes during the night and winding them up again for 6 in the morning.

In 1931 H.J.Massingham spent a year in this area writing about the Cotswolds. The Eight Bells was where he went in the evenings for "a pint of restoration" and to renew his faith in human nature, with the friendliness of the working people who frequented the pub. Mrs Molly Potter, Mr Sadler's daughter, remembers Massingham sitting in the bar eating a big piece of bread and cheese, which only cost tuppence in those days, and taking notes as the old men from the Almshouses chatted away. Massingham found rich entertainment in their stories. These are told in his book *Wold Without End.* "One night in The Eight Bells ... I learned of this champion (at shin-kicking at Dover's Games[5]) ... Nightly he would repair to The Eight Bells where his friend, armed with a coal-hammer, would 'thrape' the soft part of his shins" - in order to harden his shins for the contest.

It was in The Eight Bells that Massingham heard mention of the Ten O'Clock Tree, "a tall elm that stood on the edge of Dover's Hill and called this because the sun struck upon it at that hour. When the young corn was springing, a procession in full canonicals came to it from St James's church on 'rogation' - to bless the crops. The ceremony still lingers, though only the stump of the old tree remains."

Another of these stories concerned a shell-shocked man who "used to barricade Cider Mill Lane and cook his dinner in the middle of the road with a loaded gun on his knee. When Scuttlebrook Fair was in full swing he shot up the town on an old white horse firing right and left like a legendary outlaw from the badlands of the West, while all Campden sprinted for shelter." He was eventually lured into The Eight Bells for a pint of scrumpy and captured.

Massingham says that in November 1931 the wages of the agricultural labourer dropped to 26 shillings a week, and the beer tax emptied The Eight Bells. Mrs Molly Potter recalls that her father was a strict landlord and would not serve women in the bar; any women who in later days came with their husbands had to sit in the yard. She herself was not allowed in the bar and in fact grew up teetotal. The bar kitchen was the room at the front of the pub on the right. Here Mrs Sadler would play cards and dominoes with the older men. Behind this room was the smoke room with the bar where the younger men would play quoits, dominoes and cards. On Saturday night all the games would be put away until Monday morning, because Mr Sadler would not allow games to be played on a Sunday.

Charlie Ladbrook

The room on the left of the passageway was the club room, where the pig club would meet and its members would pay their monthly subscriptions which acted as insurance in case the pig caught some disease or died. Nearly everyone kept a pig. The pub itself kept three pigs and had pigsties backing onto the almshouses' gardens. When it was time to kill a pig, Charlie Ladbrook (the Ladbrooks were butchers) would come round. After he had killed the pig it would be salted and hung in the beer cellar. The Tiddly Club paid in sixpence or more a week here, saving for Christmas.

Many farmers made scrumpy, which the pubs would buy. Cider was stored in the skittle alley and the long upstairs room at the back of The Eight Bells would regularly be used for the sale of clothing brought by Hamilton and Bells, an Evesham shop.

A lot of cyclists would come to the pub and would sit in the yard, usually drinking tea which was served by the pub. Beer was sixpence a pint and cider twopence; and twopence also bought a packet of biscuits or crisps. The cider was drunk in china mugs, which were solid and rather square; the half-pint mug was green, the pint was white and both had a gold band round the middle. Every year on Boxing Day salted beef sandwiches, mince pies and a drink would be given to the customers.

Mr H. Griffiths, a Campdonian writing in 1947, observed that the boundaries of the various hamlets were rigorously observed in former days. The Court House, the almshouses, the vicarage and the parish church of St James are in Berrington, and the boundary line runs through the passage of The Eight Bells Inn. The boundary stone was unfortunately lost when the town was repaved in 1881. A thief arrested in Berrington could not be tried in Campden, and a special court had to be summoned in Berrington for the purpose. This was held at the Court House, hence its name. If a thief was caught running through The Eight Bells passageway, where was he tried?

The Eight Bells was owned by the brewery Whitbread Flowers until 1991 when it became a free house. It is a pub with much character.

THE ROYAL BRITISH LEGION, *Braithwaite House, High Street* 3.

Braithwaite House, a large eighteenth century house, was where C. R. Ashbee's unmarried Guildsmen lodged at the beginning of the twentieth century. The British Legion is at the back of the house, approached by a passageway. It can also be reached from Calf Lane.

Though not a pub but a club The British Legion is a place where people have enjoyed a drink for 75 years. It was formed in 1922-23 when the trustees were Major William Hart, Mr Joe Meadows, Mr Bill Bunker, Mr Fred "Stale" Benfield, Mr Bill Benfield and Mr Thomas Elsley. The Earl of Harrowby, the Rt Hon. John Dudley, originally owned Braithwaite House in the High Street, and he allowed the Legion to use it as their Headquarters. Between the wars the Mummers had their headquarters here. In 1940 the Legion bought it for £900. Subsequently the club was made bigger, the first addition being a snooker room and the main club room was completed in the early sixties. The membership is open to all over the age of 18, and there is live entertainment regularly. The club also organises various sports teams. The Royal British Legion is an organisation which helps ex-service men and women and their families when in need, and provides a social centre.

The local branch of the RAF Association also meets here. It was founded by Mr Harold Dyble, the husband of Mr Leonard Potter's daughter Grace (Mr Potter kept The Lygon Arms and the Dybles ran the Lygon in the fifties and sixties).

THE LYGON ARMS, High Street   *4.*

The Lygon Arms has a nineteenth century appearance with a central Hanoverian arched carriageway, and lunette windows on the second floor. It does, however, go back to the sixteenth century as a coaching inn. According to Rushen, in his *History ... of Chipping Campden,* the inn was originally called The White Hart. A white hart was Richard II's heraldic symbol; he insisted that all members of his household wore the device, and it would have been politic for tavern keepers to show their loyalty by displaying it. Later, it became a generic term for a tavern. The name was changed to The George during the reign of James I (1603-25). The George is mentioned in letters patent granted by James I. Presumably this name derived either from the Order of the Garter or from Saint George. In 1772 there is a reference to the inn as then called The Hare And Hounds.

There is a record of:

"A presentment made by the Jury at the Court Leet and View of the Frankpledge with the Court Barron of Sir Gerard Noel Bart., held for the said Manor [of Chipping Campden] at the usual time and place on Friday the 28th Day of October 1814.

    Before:

                George Cotterell, Gent.

                Steward there.

"....We also present John Stanley for stones lying at the Hare and Hounds door. If not removed before the fourth of November next, shall pay the sum of five shillings."

Interestingly enough the proceedings of the same Court ended with:

"We present Constables for the year ensuing: John Kingzett

                                    John Stanley."

John Stanley appears to have been collecting stone for some time, and in 1819 building works were finally carried out to The Hare And Hounds by Robert Miles for the landlord Mr Stanley, and a large amount of stone "had to Mr John Stanley for building at The Hare And Hounds Inn, Chipping Campden, found and prepared by Robert Miles." The bill was as follows:

34 loads of walling stone 2/6		£4. 5. 0.
Labour: Joseph Stanley	3 weeks 1 day	£2.17. 0.
Robert Miles	4 weeks 5 days	£3.12. 6.
W. Walters	3 days 3/4d	10.0.
John Hitchman	4 days working old stone	12.0
John Brown	4 days breaking lime stone	4.0
James Perry	3 days " " "	6.0
15 days work at walling stables at Campden		£2.5.0
Various materials used, stone mullions, timber, bills total		£78.11.4

This building work would account for the nineteenth-century appearance of the inn.

In 1821 John Stanley sold The Hare And Hounds. A bill from his solicitors, Wyatt and Tibbits, exists listing their fees for conveyancing, £48. 2s. 4d. paid by Mr William Izod in 1824 after John Stanley's death. There had been some problems. One item is 16s. 8d. for "Drawing and Ingrossing Mr Griffith's Affidavit as to the Mortgage Deeds being destroyed and the Money paid off, long and special." Also there was "a Chasm in the Title of upwards of 30 years wherein nothing appeared to have been done." So the clerk went to Evesham, "there being an Old Lady there of the Family of the name of Horne" (whose family were former owners of the inn) "about 90 years of age. Attending upon her but was not able to gain any satisfactory information." Cost: one guinea, plus horse hire and expenses 15s. 6d.

Dover's meeting in 1821 occupied two or three days, and the inns were obviously lively places during this time. One notice announced that "A main[6] of cocks will be fought each morning at Mr Thos Smith's Hare And Hounds Inn, in Campden, between the Gentlemen of Gloucestershire and Oxfordshire, to begin at ten o'clock."

Pigot & Co's *National Commercial Directory* for 1830 lists Thomas White as landlord of The Hare and Hounds, but in 1837 an old document refers to "The Hare And Hounds, now called the Lygon." There is some confusion, however, about the date when the name was changed. A handwritten notebook found at Woolstaplers Hall in the High Street states that General Lygon's butler, "Old Mullins," took over the inn about 1840, and renamed it The Lygon Arms out of sincere affection for his old master. (General Lygon fought at Waterloo and later bought the Spring Hill estate, where he is said to have planted trees in groups representing the forces drawn up at the battle of Waterloo. He belonged to the Earl of Beauchamp's family and the inn sign is the arms of the Beauchamps, two lions passant; these are surmounted by a bunch of grapes suggesting a superior establishment selling wine.) It is more likely, however, that the Woolstaplers document refers to the Broadway Lygon Arms which was part of the Spring Hill estate and also named after General Lygon, which Old Mullins certainly took over.

The 1841 census shows Thomas Dunn, aged 40, as publican living at the Lygon with his brother, Charles Dunn, who was a

The Lygon Arms

blacksmith, as Thomas Dunn was too. As there were blacksmiths here and there was a mounting stone in the courtyard the inn was probably used in the nineteenth century by visiting gentlemen who came hunting. In 1858 Slater's Directory also lists it as the Inland Revenue Office; and Morris's Commercial Directory for 1865-66 has an entry for "Inland Revenue Office, Lygon Arms. John Jones, Supervisor."

The inn was in the Dunn family until the end of the nineteenth century. The 1856 will of Mary Ann Turney, widow of James Turney, suggests that these Dunns were related to the Dunns who worked the malthouse next door to The Seymour House Hotel. The Turneys were maltsters too.

In 1884 Mrs Elizabeth Annie Dunn transferred the licence to Samuel Sambrook, a gardener at Burnt Norton House. In 1891 the Petty Sessions records show William Jeffrey as the landlord. In 1903 it was Annie Jeffrey, by which time Flowers Brewery owned it.

The Lygon Arms was let to Mr Skey on a lease for ten years from 1917. It was now known as a hotel. Norman Jewson records, in *By Chance I Did Rove*, the annual feast for the bell ringers given by F. L.

Griggs between the wars at The Lygon Arms "... in a large room normally used for farmers' ordinaries. The landlord ... whose proportions were a testimonial in themselves to a lifelong appreciation of good food and drink, proudly carved the joint, an immense sirloin, tender and juicy, cooked to a turn ... The sweet course was one of Mrs Skey's famous pies, with plenty of cream, followed by a ripe old Cheddar or Double Gloucester cheese to round off the simple but ample meal. For drink there was the best draught ale from Stratford-on-Avon in pint mugs and tankards. After toasts to the King, the bells, the host and many others had been dealt with, chairs were drawn back and the air became hazy with tobacco smoke, the tables were cleared except for fresh mugs of beer, and songs were called for ..." Mr Skey was also an undertaker and the coffins were made for him by old Tommy Taylor who lived next door in one of the two tall houses that were built with bricks left over from the railway tunnel.

In 1921 The Lygon was sold by auction (but Mr Skey remained as landlord). The poster proclaims that it has "Out offices comprising a large cellar, loose boxes and stable for six horses ... coach house or Garage ... Piggeries ... There is a Carriage Way through double doors to Baker's Lane[7]. Water laid on."

The Lygon Arms

In 1942 the Lygon was bought by Mr Leonard Potter, a local farmer, and since that time it has been owned and run by four generations of the same family. Mrs Grace Dyble, Mr Potter's daughter, ran the pub with her husband in the fifties. She was a strong character who spoke her mind. In his doctoral thesis on Chipping Campden (in the CADHAS archive) Craig Fees describes a time in 1954 when there was trouble in the town because of dances in the Town Hall which some residents claimed were noisy. One hotelier said he was packing up and leaving Campden because of the noise. One of his visitors had said that "he had not been able to get to sleep until half-past one and that the place was noisier than London." At the annual meeting of the Chamber of Trade Grace Dyble pointed out that the dances had been going on for years and said that "those residents who do not like the sound of young people enjoying themselves should shut their windows. I trust the Chamber of Trade will not be allowed to interfere with the lives of the youth of Campden and district in this manner, otherwise I can foresee the day when they will petition the vicar to have the curfew rung and have Campden all nicely tucked up and quiet by 8pm."

When the present family moved in they found that chickens had been kept on the top floor of an outbuilding behind the inn. The room where the hens had laid their eggs aloft was covered in wire netting. This area is now part of the family accommodation, the chickens having been evicted.

The Lygon Arms has remained a favourite meeting place for farmers, and over the years the Function Room has been in regular use for dances, whist drives, parties, receptions, and meetings of the local Royal and Ancient Order of Buffaloes, the Rotary Club and Hunt Meet. Skittles are still frequently played here.

The Function Room was once the stables and there were carriage houses nearby; a small cottage near to Calf Lane had previously housed a blacksmith.

Today the Lygon is a popular hotel with a restaurant and comfortable bars.

THE SWAN, High Street   5.

The Swan is a building of four storeys, with two dormer windows, a stone porch over a central doorway, and a side door to a passageway. Inside, in what is now the antique shop but was once the bar, there is a beamed ceiling and a large stone fireplace. Rushen says that The Swan was formerly two houses; the front was built when the two were made one, at the end of the eighteenth century, and it was formerly known as The Fox, a typical sign for this fox-hunting district. It was leased by John Keyt of Broadway to Thomas Garfield in 1671 for two thousand years at ten shillings rent. His son John Garfield sold the lease to Lewis Harrison in 1709. In 1780 the lease belonged to Thomas Russell, whose executors sold to Richard Hand. His widow, Anne Clarke, held it after his death in 1793 until 1830 when the children sold it to Mrs Sarah Palmer. In 1821 Mrs Clarke's tenant was James Timms; the value of the inn, stables, gardens and premises was £6, rates 3s.

The 1841 census lists Samuel Drury as innkeeper. The Drurys were a well-known family of innkeepers. In what is now Drury's Cottage, Back Ends, Henry Drury carved his name in the beams in 1864. Between 1839 and 1852 William Drury rented the right to the Booths at Dover's Hill games. In 1868 William Drury, landlord of The Swan, bought a hay-rick for ten pounds from Samuel Dunn, maltster and hop merchant-just one of the transactions involved in an innkeeper's work of providing food and

The Swan

accommodation for horses as well as people. In 1869 *The Evesham Journal* recorded that "a judge had, in a recent decision, ruled that skittles was a game and could not be allowed on licensed premises. Superintendent Monk stated that dominoes was a far greater evil. The Swan's licence was granted on condition that the skittle alley was discontinued." Later in 1869 William Drury died, and his effects were valued at £135. 19s. 11d. Amongst his effects from the brewhouse and cellar were a copper furnace, a tun pail, a six-gallon mash tub and lots of brass taps. There was also a young sow in pig and a store pig. Many innkeepers, and indeed many families, regularly kept pigs, and this continueed well into this century. Mr Fred Coldicott has memories of the pig club which met at the tithe barn (where The Tithe House stands now) opposite St James's church. The club bought pig food wholesale as well as providing insurance against the loss of a pig. William Drury left The Swan to his widow Joanna and then to his nephew William Lane.

According to *The Evesham Journal*, on 24 September 1870 Frederick Ashwin, Michael Hawley and Thomas Merriman were summoned for being drunk and riotous. Job Shervington, by then the landlord of The Swan, was required to quit for allowing them to get drunk. They were all fined a pound. On 10 December of that year there was an application for the transfer of The Swan Inn from Job Shervington to John Robert Slatter. The 1871 census lists John R.Slatter as innkeeper; perhaps he managed the pub for Joanna Drury. Kelly's Directory of 1879 lists Alfred Taplin as innkeeper. According to the 1881 census he was also a joiner, and James Osborne, hairdresser, lived there too. By 1889 there had been another change of occupancy: Kelly's names Richard Stead. In 1892 Mr J. G. Skey was landlord, and in August of that year his wife applied for a transfer of the licence, her husband being at camp with the Volunteers at Aldershot. In 1894 the Petty Sessions records show that he applied for an extension for a quadrille party at Christmas time, and again in the following April and on other occasions. (Quadrille was a popular dance which required relatively little space.)

In 1907 Norman Jewson found Campden remote and self-contained. In his book *By Chance I Did Rove* he observed, "Every other house in the High Street was, or had been, an inn, so it was not an easy matter to decide which to choose for a lodging. In the end ... I chose The Swan from its fine old sign and found I had made an excellent choice. The bar was pleasantly old-fashioned ...The inn-keeper and his wife were noted ... for making their guests comfortable, the bedrooms were unpretentious but scrupulously clean, while Mrs Skey was a first-rate cook. It was there that I first enjoyed backbone pie ..." After the pig was killed and the sides salted for bacon, the backbone was chopped into chunks, boiled with onions and sage, and then covered with pastry.

A building at the back of The Swan belonged to the Oddfellows: the name can still be seen carved in the stone. The Oddfellows were one of the three friendly societies in Campden, and their meeting room was in this building.

Mr Nevill New remembers Mr and Mrs Skey (pronounced Skee). "He was a ponderous and slow-moving man but I suppose he bustled about running the bar. Mrs Skey was a neat and precise woman. She let out perhaps three or four rooms on upper floors and made her guests most comfortable. Many of our friends stayed there if there was no room at Ivy House (where the News lived). An entry in my father's diary shows that he stayed there for two weeks in August 1914. We were all on holiday but my father had to curtail his holiday because of the war so he stayed at The Swan until the rest of us came home." Several pubs in Campden were closed at the end of the war, but The Swan apparently closed voluntarily so that the premises could be used by the school. For Nevill New "The Swan was the greatest loss among the closed pubs."

In 1919 The Swan belonged to the Grammar School and classes were held there, carrying on until the new Grammar School was built in 1928; after this domestic science classes still took place here until 1946 when the building became the main teaching block for the Campden School of Arts and Crafts, which held an annual exhibition in the building behind The Swan. In the fifties the Youth Club was held on the top two floors of The Swan. The Grammar School sold The Swan after the new comprehensive school was built in the sixties.

Today The Swan is an antique shop, with the swan sign hanging outside.

THE SHAKESPEARE HOTEL, Cheltenham House, High Street   6.

This is now the Oxford Shirt Shop. There is the trace of an old carriageway arch above the side door and incorporated into the shop window. An early twentieth-century photograph shows the sign of The Shakespeare Hotel and Garage outside Cheltenham House, but there is no reference to this in the deeds.

The Shakespeare Hotel

22

This is now Stuart Antiques. Inside there are beams and a large fireplace.

The Live and Let Live was hopefully named, but that hope was not always fulfilled: John Lane, the landlord in 1863, was often in trouble with the local police sergeant William Bird, who it seems did not want to live and let live, making three attempts that year to put a stop to John Lane's merriment. On 19 February 1863 a summons was served on John Lane: Sgt Bird alleged that he "did knowingly permit disorderly conduct ... by then and there suffering persons to the number of twelve and more to remain fighting, drinking and making a great noise and disturbance there at a late hour of the night, to wit, about three o'clock in the morning." The next week, 25 February, it was claimed by Sgt Bird that John Lane

The Live and Let Live

"did knowingly permit Drunkenness and other disorderly conduct." On 4 March 1863 Sgt Bird struck again, with another summons: John Lane was accused, "You did knowingly suffer Gaming in your said House ... there permitting one Alexander Payne and three other persons to play for Ale at Cards." (Alexander Payne was a cooper, and sexton at St James's Church.) In the notes for his defence on all three counts John Lane's solicitor commented, "A Publican can keep open his House at night provided he maintains good order. Dancing is not an offence, except in the Metropolis and within twenty miles of it ... Mr Lane had a Ball at his house on Ash Wednesday instead of Christmas. He naturally provided a card-table for those who could not dance, but only playing for money makes cards unlawful ... Playing at cards is not an unlawful Game within the meaning of the Alehouse Act."

In 1867 Morris's Commercial Directory mentions John Lane as "beer retailer and tobacconist." In the 1871 census John Lane, aged 41, was still the innkeeper, and indeed the deeds show that he was still there in 1889, so Sgt Bird evidently did not manage to suppress him. On 10 October 1889 John Lane conveyed The Live and Let Live to Hunt Edmunds and Co. of Banbury, wine merchants, for £600. The property was then in two parts: the main building (now Stuart Antiques) and two cottages of which one was formerly a blacksmith's shop (this is the little house between Stuart House and Cheltenham House), "all of which was recently converted into one tenement by John Lane, known as The Live and Let Live Inn." The Petty Sessions records show that in 1891 John Harris was landlord and in 1903 it was John Keen. Hunt Edmunds and Co. kept the inn for 32 years, and then in 1921 conveyed it to Thomas Elsley for £450. Thomas Elsley had lived in the adjoining property, Cheltenham House, since 1912. He now expanded his business as ironmonger, seedsman, stationer and later newsagent, joining The Live and Let Live premises, no longer an inn, to his original shop.

The Live and Let Live was closed at the end of the first world war. At the Campden Petty Sessions it was said that supervision was difficult for the landlord, as the cellar and the kitchen were below the level of the front part. The landlord, Mr Fairweather, said this was no inconvenience. He also supplied newspapers to be read on the premises. But the court took the view that the news could be found at other houses, and the licence was not renewed.

Mr Nevill New remembers, "This was run by Mr and Mrs Fairweather. I have little recollection of him but Mrs Fairweather was a rather buxom woman, and as a sideline she boiled and prepared tripe in a little shop which must have been attached to the pub. She also sold

Joey Fairweather

24

brawn. My mother often bought tripe from her and it was delicious."
Mrs Sue Durrant remembers her father telling her that one day when the
pub had opened at 5.30 in the morning (as the pubs did to provide for
the farm workers and other early risers) and the first customer appeared
just before closing time, Joe Fairweather said, "I haven't served anyone
all day, and I'm not going to start now."

In 1930 Elsley sold off what had been the main portion of The Live
and Let Live premises to Christopher Whitfield, described as "company
director" but well known now as the Campden historian. He
manufactured metal bedsteads in Birmingham. Whitfield covenanted
not to use his new property for the business of an ironmonger or
newsagent for ten years; Elsley covenanted not to use his property as a
drapery for the same period. Presumably Whitfield intended to open a
draper's shop. In the late thirties there was a restaurant here called The
Live and Let Live, for which Mr Allan Warmington's father, Mr Joe
Warmington, made a new oak sign; the restaurant only lasted for a few
years.

At different times there was a shoe shop here, a draper's, a barber's,
and a sweet shop. Mrs Agnes Allard ran her greengrocery from
Cheltenham House in the thirties. More recently, before Stuart
Antiques, there was a fashionable dress shop here.

THE OLD KING'S ARMS, *Caminetto, High Street* 8.

This is a sixteenth-century building, timber-framed with two gables
and an overhanging first floor, which, if it was indeed there in the
sixteenth century, protected the ground floor when chamber pots were
emptied from first-floor windows but was hazardous for passers-by. The
wrought iron heraldic sign is by Griggs.

In 1821 the Campden Ratebook has an entry for "The King's Arms
Inn & stables and garden etc. value £9 rates 4s/6d." The owner occupier
was Richard Andrews. William Toft was Publican in 1841. In 1858
Slater's Directory lists Joseph Bloxham as landlord. *The Evesham
Journal* of 23 November 1869 recorded that "On Sunday afternoon last
a boy named Harwood was playing in a dungheap in The King's Arms
yard, which from the recent rain was converted into an immense slough.
From some cause or other the little boy was drowned. At the inquest Mr
Brace, the landlord, said the hole (through which the child had entered)
was new and not yet completed; the door was not yet on. He was willing

to make whatever amendment the coroner recommended." In 1881 Thomas Brace was still Innkeeper, and tailor. He was the last landlord of the old King's Arms. He had a reputation for strong ale; after his death large quantities of horsemeat were found in the vats, which no doubt explained the potency of his drink.

The Old King's Arms as the Technical School

In the 1871 census, Phoenix Place (as it is now called), formerly Lodging House Yard, is known as King's Arms Yard. The lodging house there was run by Hanna Toft, the wife of the former landlord William, and catered for some of the workers on the railway.

In 1891 at the Petty Sessions the King's Arms licence was not renewed; a superintendent of police gave evidence to the effect that there were seven full licensed houses within 435 yards, a beer house next door, and two grocers licensed in the street. He added moreover, "The premises are in a dilapidated condition, not fit for a public house in their present state... the house is not required. This is my opinion. It wants pulling down."

Later that year Canon Bourne, trustee and governor of the school nearby, succeeded in getting the County Council to provide £700 for the purchase of The King's Arms Inn. With a grant from the County Council it was converted into a technical school which considerably extended the Grammar School's curriculum. The premises were ready in 1893 and there were evening classes open to the public, which a large number of agricultural labourers are said to have attended. There were demonstration lectures on dairying, veterinary classes and cookery classes. The options also included shorthand, nursing, chemistry, drawing and woodcarving. It is interesting that before C. R. Ashbee arrived with the Guild of Handicraft, Campden was already offering a variety of technical and practical courses. The Technical School did, however, prove useful to Campden School of Arts and Crafts at the beginning of the twentieth century. In 1919 Grammar School classes were still being held here. The Grammar School sold The King's Arms in 1928. Jewson altered the building in 1929, when he either

The Old King's Arms after its restoration by Jewson in 1929

created or restored the overhang. Previously there had been a flat Victorian brick façade.

In the early thirties The King's Arms became a tea room. In 1935 it moved across the High Street to what had been Ardley House and became a hotel. The old King's Arms kept a restaurant called the King's Arms Pantry. At some time the building was a photographer's. The Freemasons have their temple upstairs. Now it houses Caminetto, a restaurant and bistro with beamed ceilings, exposed stone walls and an attractive atmosphere.

THE NOEL ARMS HOTEL, High Street   9.

The main block is eighteenth-century ashlar. To the left it has a nineteenth-century oriel window and a carriage entrance.

The Noel Arms was originally a private residence, perhaps fourteenth century. Rushen mentions that John Wilson is said to have held about

27

1712 a messuage, dove house, garden and orchard, and Pear Tree Close. These premises may be those now known as The Noel Arms Hotel. Until the early nineteenth century The Noel Arms was known as The George, and the sign earlier used by The Lygon Arms was transferred to The Noel Arms when this became a hotel. The lane behind The Noel Arms Hotel is called George Lane. This was a packhorse track which ran under The Noel Arms archway, and was used by packhorse trains carrying wool from Campden to Bristol and Southampton.

In 1788 The George was where legal business was carried out. In September of that year John Hughes of Stretton wrote to Mr Cottrell, a lawyer whose activities are recorded in the Cottrell papers (in the CADHAS archives), "I received a line from Mr William Sheldon last Thursday to spend that evening with him at The George Inn. After supper I shewed him Mr W's marriage settlement."

The Universal British Directory, 1793-98, describing Campden, comments: "The principal inn is The George. There is a waggon from London for this place from The Bull and Mouth near Aldersgate-street every Wednesday and Saturday at eleven in the morning."

At the end of the eighteenth century the enclosure of land led to appeals about bridleways and public footpaths. These appeals would have generated some of the passions now associated with appeals against motorways and ring roads. In 1799 Meetings of the Enclosure Commissioners appointed to hear such appeals all took place at the George Inn. For example, a record exists of one such meeting there on 30th September 1799 where they

> "Heard Appeal against the Bridle Road leading from Broad Campden to Blockley over the cow pasture fields to the gate entring the Hamlet of Northwick at the Corner of Northwick Park Wall and the arguments adduced for making the same a public Carriage Road when it was thought advisable that the same should be set out as a public Carriage & Drift[8] Road of the Breadth of 40 Feet and the Surveyors were directed to stake out the same accordingly."

They continued to sit until 10 October, and fixed their next meeting for 2 December at the same place - so they were evidently satisfied with their accommodation. J. P. Nelson in his book on Chipping Campden refers to this, and thinks The George was probably The George and Dragon. The Noel Arms, however, was named The George at this date, and the appeals are more likely to have been heard there.

It was still called The George in 1810 when the Rev. Elisha Smith, Baptist Minister in Campden, held a meeting on 3 June for the Oxford Association of Particular Baptist churches and "upward of seventy persons dined at The George."

The Noel Arms

By 1821, however, the name had changed. The 1821 Campden Ratebook lists "The Noels (sic) Arms Inn, & Malthouse, Bowling Green, Buildings and premises. Value £25, rates 12s/6d." The Proprietor was the Hon.C. N. Noel, and the tenant was John Berry. Pigot's Directory of 1830 lists "The Noel Arms (Posting)" with James Turney as landlord. The Noel family had been (and still is) closely associated with Chipping Campden since Sir Baptist Hicks's daughter, Lady Juliana, married Edward Noel, Baron Noel of Kidlington. Sir Baptist Hicks died in 1629 without any male heir, so the title of Viscount Campden passed to Edward Noel, whose grandson became the first Earl of Gainsborough. The manor has descended continuously through the Noel family to the present day.

In *The Diary of a Cotswold Parson,* the Rev. F. E. Witts notes in August 1836, "At Campden we bated our horse at the principal Inn [presumably The Noel Arms], a very clean and neat place.... Campden is a dull, clean, disused market town."

In 1844 the landlord was Hugh Mullins, and the inn was the excise office as well as the posting house.

In the seventeenth century and later, tokens were issued by shops and inns to relieve the shortage of small coins. They were of value only at the establishments that issued them. Several tokens of this date have been found in Campden, and as late as 1850 The Noel Arms issued tokens.

In 1858 Slater's Directory lists John Wyatt as landlord, but in 1859 the Bristol Post Office Directory has John Cousins as licensee.

The Noel Arms was an important coaching inn; in the courtyard outside steps can still be seen which were used by the coachmen after seeing to their horses so that they would not disturb the other guests, who had exclusive use of the front door. Mr Allan Warmington remembers that the public bar at the back of the hotel had "Ostler" written over the door.

The 1871 and 1881 censuses list Mark Gurton as innkeeper. He was a local cricketer who captained a successful team against Shipston, commemorated in an anonymous poem in the CADHAS archive, "The Shipstoniad." As his team prepares for the combat,

Gurton's castle yard is rife
With varied scenes of bustling life

The Noel Arms Courtyard

- his castle yard being, of course, the courtyard of The Noel Arms.

In 1873, according to *The Evesham Journal,* Mr Gurton "bet he would walk fair heel and toe from his house, to a spot on the Draycott to Moreton road known as the Dorn turn, within the hour, being a distance of fully five miles and anything but a good road, there being more than one steep hill. Mr John Rimell from Wold's End was starter and judge. He did it just short of fifty minutes humming as he went along "Britons never will be slaves."

In 1889 Kelly's Directory names Albert Tanner. While he was innkeeper The Noel Arms advertised itself: "Posting House. Billiards and Smoke Rooms. Broughams, Carriages and Traps for hire. Agents for Great Western Railway. Omnibus meets every train. Albert Tanner, proprietor." Albert Tanner was noted for his malapropisms; Mr W. H. Warmington recalled how he announced his wife's *accouchement* as her "encroachment." Ben Benfield, Ben the Bus, worked for Albert Tanner driving the omnibus to the station. He did the same for Mr Tanner's successor, Mr H.J.Berry.

The Noel Arms had an Assembly Room, the upstairs room with the oriel window. This very large room was later divided into several bedrooms, of which the one with the oriel window is now a splendid four-poster bedroom. When the Assembly Room existed it was the standard venue for meetings and official dinners in Campden; for example, in 1880 the Rifle Corps Dinner, the Britannia Benefit Club Dinner, the Lighting Inspectors' Annual Vestry Meeting, and the General Meeting of the North Cotswold Farmers' Association were all held here. Almost anything involving the Earl of Gainsborough and the Noel family took place here too. In 1889 a Volunteer Ball took place here and according to *The Evesham Journal,*

"The room was most tastefully decorated. At the end over the oriel window was a large shield emblazoned with flags, whilst at the opposite end of the room appeared the loyal motto, 'God Save the Queen.' The sides and end of the room were embellished with a light wreath of ivy hanging in festoons, with flags, pictures, and crossed bayonets, under which was the handsomely decorated legend in letters of gold, 'At rest, but ready.'

"Dancing commenced shortly after 9 o'clock, to the strains of Wheatley's Quadrille Band (Evesham), and was continued with unflagging spirit till 4 a.m."

In 1890 an opera "Caliph" was organised by Father Lloyd and presented there. The Petty Sessions records show that several times, for example in December 1893, and again in January and December 1897 and in May 1898, Mr Tanner applied for an extension for a private quadrille party. Frequently balls were held here. In May 1906 an occasional licence was granted to Albert Tanner to sell alcohol in a tent in the old court orchard (behind the Court House in Calf Lane) at the Whit Monday Fête, from 1 to 10 p.m.

In the early years of the twentieth century a travelling theatre family called Holloways came to the Noel yard and set up a theatre tent for two to three months. They performed a number of plays to big audiences. The actors lived in caravans in the yard. In the 1930s and after the war The Osiris Players, a women's theatre group based in Willersey, who performed Shakespeare around the area, travelling in a white Rolls Royce, put on their plays in the Noel Arms courtyard and outbuildings. In 1947 Nancy Hewins, the leader, played Falstaff in Campden.

An annual cattle show and sale was also held in the sale yard behind The Noel courtyard in the 1930s. Railings which formed part of the cattle pens can still be seen. Until the 1950s, when both markets ceased to operate, the cattle and pig market was held there too, and the regular sheep market was held in The Square. Part of the site behind The Noel (to the right of the archway, entering from the High Street) was the town bowling green, until its sad demise in 1989. The last bowls match was played against Northwick Park, the Blockley team, Campden's old foes, on Saturday 16 September.

This hotel was the last in Campden to brew its own beer. The landlord, Charlie Wakeman from Birmingham, employed Percy Dewey, son of the school teacher, to brew beer. He was a renowned story-teller, telling stories in dialect on the radio and inspiring many of H. J. Massingham's tales, told in *Wold Without End*. Percy Dewey, the painter Captain Hudson with his wooden leg, and Chris Whitfield, the historian of Campden, were a high-spirited trio who drank at the Noel and played pranks on Charlie Wakeman. The latter's love of old things was great, but his knowledge of them was not. Mr Fred Coldicott tells how the three took a chamber pot, muddied it, and wrote around the rim in "old lettering": TOPIS SINTO. They then buried it in the garden of the Noel, "found" it, and presented it to Charlie, who was very excited, believing the inscription to be Latin and the object medieval.

Today The Noel Arms, which is privately owned, is a pleasant hotel with a restaurant, oak-beamed bars and a conservatory. It has an attractive large fireplace serving two rooms with stone inglenook seats.

THE RED LION, High Street   10.

The Red Lion was once on the upper side of the street, in Leysbourne, not its present site. It is referred to in a 1640 deed to Pretty's House (where Leasebourne House is now). Robert Taylor then inherited "Pretty's House in Laisborn" and "a messuage on the upper side of the street there ... known as The Redde Lyon." The name must have moved

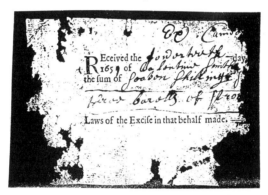

Brewery receipts found in the Red Lion Chipping Campden during alterations made in April 1929, for the payment in 1659-1661 of excise on beer at the rate of half a crown a barrel.

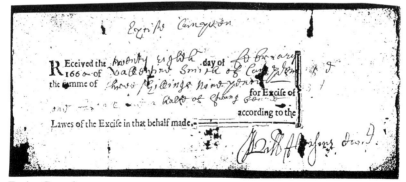

Excise Campden
Received the twenty eigth day of February 1660 of Valentine Smith of Campden the sums of three shillings nine pence for excise of one barrel and halfe of strong bears (beers) according to the lawes of the excise in that behalf made.
Will Persons commissioner

33

before 1659 as there are receipts for the present Red Lion of that date.

The present Red Lion buildings go back to the sixteenth century. With its red lion sign, it has flagged floors, low ceilings, a huge inglenook fireplace with stone seats and a paved yard leading behind the pub to an exit in Sheep Street. Rushen says it boasts a licensed history as old as any in the town. There are receipts for tax paid on beer going back to 1659. In 1723 it was kept by one Lodge Knight, who owned it. Later it was in the hands of the Walford family. A Mr Tomes bought The Red Lion in 1780 and sold it to George Manton in 1808, when, however, it was a private dwelling house. Not many years later it was again licensed. In 1821 the Campden Ratebook lists The Red Lion Inn with gardens stables and premises value £14, rates 7s. Mrs Richards was the proprietor and Thomas Usher the tenant. In 1830 Thomas Usher is still listed as innkeeper; in 1841 William Smith; in 1858, according to Slater's Directory, it was James Gibson, and he was still there in 1894. Produce was often sold in the yard. Today the fish van calls there every Friday.

James Holtam was there in 1910; Mrs Ellen Bridge took over after the first world war, when The Rose and Crown was closed down, while her husband John was with the army in France, and he joined her later. One of the first things the family did was to throw out the brass spittoons. There was reputedly one old man who could spit right across the bar with good aim. He presumably missed the old spittoons.

Sid Bridge, son of Ellen and John, then took over and when he was in the army in the second world war Mrs Ellen Bridge, now a widow, ran the pub, and Sid took over again on his return and ran the pub with his wife Lillian. Mrs Sue Durrant, Sidney's granddaughter, relates how one night Sidney and his friend Alec Cooper were in the cellar having a crafty late tipple. His wife Lily decided to call a halt to their binge. She got out of bed and went down to the cellar. Alec looked up with a shocked expression and said, "Cor, Mrs Bridge, I thought you was a bloomin' angel!" Travellers came in summer time but were only served at the cellar door, and only for a certain length of time. One woman traveller knocked on the door and asked for another drink after the allotted time. Sidney told Lily to go and say they weren't serving any more. The miffed traveller said to Lily, "Mrs Bridge, you're an old witch, but your husband's a perfect gentleman." Lily retold the story and laughed: "It was the perfect gentleman who sent the old witch to throw her out."

Charlie Ladbrook with his brother Lawrence would kill pigs and joint them for people in the yard. Mr Jack Clarke had the pub from 1968 to 1969, when it was taken over by C. L. Moule. Mr Keith Moule became landlord in 1972 until 1990, the pub then belonging to the Bass brewery in Birmingham, who had refurbished it in the sixties. In the eighties legislation to restrict monopolies meant that the brewery sold it; fortunately The Red Lion, like The Eight Bells, was bought as a pub.

George Hart, the son of George Henry Hart[9] the Guild silversmith, and well known as Jethro Larkin in The Archers, was a Red Lion regular, with his own special corner at the pub.

When Jean and Bob Wilson refurbished the pub in 1991 they found

The Red Lion

old coins, the oldest one of which dated back to 1762. They also found an old ecclesiastical stone head, which has now been fixed above the fireplace.

At the rear of The Red Lion, in the yard, the first garage in Campden was built, in wood, in 1921. Mr William Cutts, who had trained in the Rolls-Royce works, became the chauffeur at The Noel Arms, driving the omnibus to the station to collect visitors. He decided Campden needed a garage, and started one at The Red Lion. In his book Mr Fred Coldicott tells the story of the foreman, Mr Bates, stealing wood from Corporation houses which he was building in Aston Road and selling it to William Cutts. Mr Bates was sent to prison.

The Red Lion, an inn full of character, continues to serve the town today.

THE ROYAL OAK, Royal Oak Terrace, Sheep Street 11.

The corner cottage in Royal Oak Terrace at right angles to the road was probably the pub. Mr H. Griffiths, writing in 1947, remembered The Royal Oak "probably dating from the days of Charles II - for Campden was always royalist and loyal - and the cottage next to it was another inn named The Bush. If mine host of The Royal Oak had annoyed a customer he transferred his attention to The Bush; till he, perhaps inadvertently, kicked over the traces there - when that happened, he would return to The Royal Oak. It would have been a continuous atmosphere of Montagues and Capulets. In those far-off days there was no early closing of pubs, and beer was locally home-brewed."

It is said that The Royal Oak was a cider house.

THE BUSH, Royal Oak Terrace, Sheep Street   12.

See The Royal Oak, above. The name derives from the custom (dating back to Roman times) of displaying a bush over the door of a house selling wine or ale; hence the saying, "Good wine needs no bush." It was a Campden custom for revellers at Dover's Games to place a bush of oak outside the doors of important residents and to call there for drink later on. Not surprisingly, this practice was not universally popular, and died out.

THE ELM, Lower High Street   13.

Rushen mentions The Elm as a beerhouse. The Elm was the house on the corner of Sheep Street next to The Plough and now Robert Welch's shop. Stephen Whatcote (sometimes Whatcott), who lived here in the 1860s, was a beer retailer. He subsequently bought The Plough next door. Petty Sessions records of 1887 show The Elm applying for an extension for the 21st June, along with eight other pubs. No other reference to The Elm has been found.

THE PLOUGH, Lower High Street   14.

The Plough is now a private house next to Robert Welch's shop; the pub also occupied part of Robert Welch's shop. It has a gable and mullioned windows and dates back to the early seventeenth century. A list of all who could bear arms in 1608 includes the innkeeper of The Plough, John Jenks, a musketeer. In 1796 Edward Woodward died in the island of Martinique, leaving the Plough Inn to his younger brother. So it would appear that The Plough had been an inn from early days, but the first mention of it as an inn in the deeds is not until 1873, when Stephen

Whatcote, who already owned The Elm (the house on the corner next to The Plough), bought The Plough and the Bridge Garden, a garden in Watery Lane (now called Park Road), for £240. Stephen Whatcote was beerhouse keeper, butcher and shopkeeper. After his death an inventory of his effects includes:

Brew House: Mash tub, 4 coolers, copper furnace, sieve, stirrer.

Cellar: 7 Beer Hogsheads.

Stable: 2 cider barrels.

Grocer's shop: Deal counter and shelves, 2 small sets of scales and weights, 7 tea canisters.

Room over shop: Sausage machine and grinder.

The Plough on the corner opposite the old Elm Tree and The Rose and Crown

His daughters inherited The Plough, though his widow Elizabeth ran it. In 1898 they sold it along with The Elm to Hunt, Edmunds & Co. of Banbury for £110. it is said that the Plough sign ended up as a wooden seat for an earth closet at the back of cottages in Sheep Street. The brewery kept the premises for thirty years until 1928, but The Plough lost its licence in 1919. The licensee was a widow, Mrs Starkiss, who appealed at the Campden Petty Sessions. She was entirely dependent on the business, with no son and two daughters. But it was objected that all the rooms were dark, there was no Bottle and Jug, no stable, an indoor W.C. but no urinal, and only one entrance. The purchaser in 1928 was F.L.Griggs, who bought it for the Campden trust, which proceeded to renovate the building. Several inns were renovated by Norman Jewson in 1929.

Mr Fred Coldicott remembers Mrs Starkiss as the last landlady. She moved to a cottage in Watery Lane where from a shed in her garden she sold sweets. Since then The Plough has been a bakery run by the Calloways and then Mr Cyril James, an antique shop and a craft shop.

THE HARROW INN,
now Harrow House, Further Afield, Lower High Street 15.

Harrow House has two dormer windows, stone mullioned windows with hood moulds, and a Tudor style doorway. It is now a private house. Until 1986 Mr Seumas Stewart had his well-known antiquarian bookshop "Serif" here.

There is no evidence in the deeds, but people say The Harrow was a beerhouse at the beginning of the twentieth century and Whitfield mentions it. It was opposite the large elm tree (no longer there) which was the hiring place for agricultural workers, so it was appropriate that The Plough and The Harrow should be the two pubs nearest the spot. Trees where workers assembled to offer themselves for employment were known as "Hiring Trees." There were similar trees at Broad Campden, Mickleton and Blockley, and the Hiring was often accompanied by stalls and amusements. In 1872 a meeting was held under the Elm Tree to form an agricultural union. An old farm labourer called Job Benfield was called upon to preside and he complained about conditions and about the "lingering not living" he had done. The new agricultural unions met under the tree and it was known as the Union Tree. Because the unions sought to reform the conditions of agricultural workers, in 1895 the Bristol Observer referred to the tree as the Reformers Tree. In the 1870s it was also known as the Gospel Tree, because religious services were conducted there. In 1873 The Evesham Journal wrote about a case in which it was alleged that "the defendants were using the most blasphemous language on the Sunday evening during the time the Rev. H. Noel was holding open-air service under the Elm Tree." A case was heard in 1899 in which a Methodist evangelist lay-preacher was convicted for "shouting" on several nights beneath the Elm Tree. He spoke so loudly that, it was testified, several persons were taken ill in their houses, and according to one man, it seemed to "perce right thro' you." A new law against public noise seems to have brought to an end the use of the old Elm Tree as a place of assembly and a "speakers' corner".

THE ROSE AND CROWN, Lower High Street   16.

The Rose and Crown is now a private house. It is a seventeenth-century building with two gables, mullioned windows with hood moulds, and a Tudor style doorway with an oak door. The Brewhouse near to it has very similar windows and was possibly part of the old pub.

The Rose and Crown was a Tudor inn sign indicating loyalty to the monarch, but it is very doubtful if the pub itself had a very old licensed history. The 1838-64 deeds of Elm Tree House mention The Rose and Crown. In 1838 Benjamin Blakeman occupied The Rose and Crown; in 1843 Michael Howley; in 1853 Thomas Howley; in 1864 Frederick Phipps. At the Petty Sessions in October 1871 The Rose and Crown was transferred from Phipps to John Hartwell; the superintendent of police said Hartwell was a timber and coal dealer. The applicant here interposed that he had done a bit of anything and something of nothing for a living. The chairman said, "Don't you think you could do better than keep a public house?" Hartwell said, "I will keep my house as it ought to be and if the company don't keep themselves right I'll stop the tap." The application was granted. Later that year, at the annual Mop, John Hartwell roasted a pig outside The Rose and Crown, but attendance at the fair was very low, and it was said to be "one of the dullest statutes."[10]

On 30 May 1874 there was a serious fire at The Rose and Crown; a chimney fire ignited two beams, which apparently had smouldered all day and night. It burst into flames in The Rose and Crown and the neighbouring house, the property of J. Rimell and J. Haydon. C. Ladbrook, J. Keen, B. Sharp and Supt. McRae all helped to control the fire.

In 1881 John Waine was the innkeeper. In 1891 it was Fred Timms, but sadly in 1903 he cut his throat with a razor, and died a few hours later. His wife of six months said he was in good health but was being treated for internal pains. Four weeks before he had lost his horse, but a little over £3 had been collected for him towards another. Timms was found in the washhouse with a razor. Supt. Jones and Dr Dewhurst came but they could not save him. Short Ann Bennett (there being a tall Ann Bennett) laid him out.

Mr Fred Coldicott remembers The Rose and Crown closed at the time of the first world war. This was the favourite pub of "Slap" Blakeman (so called because he slapped his whip against his thigh), famous boozer and colt-breaker, who lived in a cottage up behind Old Poplars Farm. As a result of these two occupations he had broken nearly every bone in his body at some time. One leg was badly crippled, but when the doctor told him it was "old age" he replied, with his characteristic stammer, "The other b-b-b-bugger's all right and it's exactly the same age." Slap got a local lad to push him in a basketwork wheelchair. The regular itinerary was The Rose and Crown, The Volunteer, round Back Ends to The Eight Bells in Church Street. One evening, coming down the slope of Back Ends to the Aston Road, the lad let go of the chair, and Slap rolled onto the main road, where he overturned and fell out. Under his rug he had a bottle for urinating in as he progressed round the town, and in his mishap this was broken. A charitable old lady, Miss Griffiths, known as the Angel of Campden, always kind to the poor, witnessed his accident and rushed to help him. "I'm not hurt," he said, "but" - waving the broken urine bottle - "I've lost all my whisky." She gave him the money for a replacement.

On another occasion, according to Mr Allan Warmington, Slap was driving some people home in his cart. Very drunk, he whipped up his horse, shouting, "Have you ever been thrown out? You're going to be tonight." Another night, over his cups, Slap sold someone a donkey for five pounds. The next day the man came to him complaining, "That donkey you sold me is dead." Slap replied, "I thought it was when I saw it in the field this morning."

In 1918 The Rose and Crown, then known as a cider house, was one of six pubs that lost their licences. Mrs Ellen Bridge, the licensee, pleaded at the Petty Sessions that her husband had been in the Army during the war. She had three children and her husband was now in France. She was dependent on the licence. Trade was good, there were club meetings fortnightly with fifty-eight members. But the police objected that the entrance to the stables was through the house, there was no Jug and Bottle, the urinal was rough, and there was poor accommodation for the licensee. Hitchman & Co., who owned the pub, said the Company held an option of purchase on an adjoining property, and if the Bench thought it desirable would exercise that option to improve the private part of the premises. The outcome was that Mrs Bridge lost her licence, but on the vicar's advice went to see the owner of The Red Lion, and took that on, making a deal with the brewery.

THE VOLUNTEER, St Catharine's Square   *17.*

The Volunteer has an archway through to a pleasant courtyard and garden, and it has a cosy and welcoming bar. It was almost certainly a beerhouse in the middle of the eighteenth century, but its name is not known. In 1853 the deeds refer to this building as a dwelling house, belonging to Emanuel Tomes, a builder. Ten years later it was occupied by Richard Griffin, described as "Licensed Victualler", who was about to purchase it for himself. The conveyance refers to "a public house known by the sign as The Volunteer." For a thousand years, since Alfred the Great made all his subjects soldiers, every town in England had to find men to bear arms. First the Sheriff, then the Lord Lieutenant raised the Militia. For centuries this was done haphazardly. Eventually a set county quota was raised by ballot and every parish registered its able men aged 18 to 45. Those chosen served for five years. They later came to be known as Volunteers. The Volunteer movement was reorganised in 1859, so the first use of the name The Volunteer probably dates from 1859 when the volunteers came to the inn to sign on; the inn may have been known by a different name sometime between 1853 and 1859. (It figures as The Rifle Volunteer in Morris's Commercial Directory of 1867.)

The Volunteer

41

Richard Griffin was evidently left short of cash as a result of his purchase, and lost no time in raising funds by means of a mortgage. Five days after acquiring the inn he mortgaged it for £300 to Henry Lardner, brewer, of Little Compton. He never succeeded in clearing this debt, and eighteen years later sold out to his mortgagee.

It was in Richard Griffin's time as licensee that Queen Victoria's Golden Jubilee was celebrated in 1887, when the procession marched from The Eight Bells to The Volunteer and then drank and dined in the market square. Richard Griffin was also driver of the station bus (a horse-drawn vehicle). He wore a coaching coat and curly-brimmed black beaver. He died sometime before 1897.

In 1898 the Compton Steam Brewery Sale (see The Eight Bells) included The Volunteer, which had been one of its tied houses: "An attractive stone and slated house with good frontage to the main street, six Bed Rooms and two staircases ... Garden with Cistern House, Pigsties and W.C. ... Also a cottage adjoining with garden in rear, W.C. and Coal House." Ownership passed to Flowers Brewery.

In 1902 the licence was transferred from Charles Aston to Thomas Malin of Stratford-on-Avon. In the 1920s the landlord was Mr Rathbone; he had a garage at the side of the inn. Ray Turner, Rathbone's son-in-law, followed him, and was landlord for 24 years, until George Arthurs took over in 1962. George Arthurs and his son Tony were the landlords for the next seventeen years, until 1979, when Whitbread Flowers sold the inn to Bernard Harris, and it once again became a free house. On Christmas Eve in many years the Mummers, who performed their plays in pubs and houses, played in The Volunteer Inn. The cast included Father

The Volunteer

Christmas, Bold Slasher, King George, the Doctor, the Drummer, Jack Vinney, Fiddler Crump, and Beelzebub. Today the mumming still takes place here and in other pubs.

During the second world war, when American soldiers were drinking in The Volunteer, Sal Botheridge, who normally drank at the lid holes, would go inside the pub with empty bottles tucked inside her jacket. As the soldiers bought her drinks she tipped them into her bottles and so went away with more than she could have consumed on the spot. (Sal was a well-known figure at any auction of goods in town, and would always bid one shilling for everything, and then sell things on, sometimes before the auction was finished. At one auction Mr Bower, the auctioneer, called out, "Now Sal, am I selling things or are you?")

Mrs Hilary Sinclair bought the inn in 1985 with her son Paul. The present inn sign features the badge of the Gloucestershire Regiment. This Regiment fought at the Battle of Alexandria in Egypt on 21 March 1801, against the French. Napoleon was on his way to India with the intention of dominating the Middle East. During the battle the French cavalry broke through, and the Gloucesters were ordered to turn round and fight back to back. They won the battle and also the right to wear their badges on the front and back of their headgear.

THE GREEN DRAGON, *Green Dragons, Lower High Street 18.*

This is a seventeenth-century house with mullioned and transomed windows. The date 1691 is on the façade, but the sundial in the gable is dated 1647. A 1674 document in the Earl of Northampton's archives certifies Mrs Katherine Owen of The Green Dragon to be in good health, so it seems the inn was functioning then. In 1682 a visitation of heralds stayed here and according to Mr Robert Noel, of the Royal College of Heralds, they left bills and receipts at Green Dragons showing that they had run up a substantial expense account, eating, drinking and being merry. In 1803 the earliest deed shows the property belonging to Charles, Earl of Northampton: an inn "called or commonly known by the name of The Green Dragon" with the barn, stables, yard and garden, then in the occupation of John Baldwin. On 28 March 1707 a meeting was held at the inn by the Bishop of Gloucester to discuss the first-fruits and tithes in certain livings; the inn must have been an important one.

During the Dover's Hill Games of 1808 there was "a main of cocks fought each morning between the Gentlemen of Gloucestershire and

Green Dragons formely The Green Dragen

Worcestershire." In *A History of Chipping Campden* Whitfield says that "the cockpit was removed from The Green Dragon in 1924 when the inn was converted into a private house." But in fact it seems that The Green Dragon had ceased to be an inn by 1821 when the Campden Ratebook listed the "late Green Dragon Inn." Nathan Smith purchased the property in 1827. In the document of that transaction there is an intriguing reference to a "chapel". Another reference of interest is in the 1914 deed, to "the building at the rear known as the Banqueting House." The Marquess of Northampton sold the inn in December 1818 to John Nailor, yeoman, of Campden, for £420. John Crockett was now the landlord.

When Nathan Smith purchased The Green Dragon in 1827 it was occupied by him as his residence. He then divided the property into two dwellings and leased to Samuel Wheatley, shopkeeper, a messuage "formerly part of The Green Dragon Inn together with the chapel, pigsties, carthouses, and the right of way ... through a certain close now in the occupation of Nathan Smith." In 1830 Richard Hall, Nathan Smith's nephew, sold The Green Dragon to James Turney of Broadway; he died in 1855, leaving it to his widow Mary Ann Turney. In 1856 The Green Dragon was auctioned at the Lygon Arms and the highest bidder was John Wyatt, butcher. The properties were described as two messuages and a butcher's shop. In 1859 John Wyatt was declared bankrupt. He was then described as "licensed victualler, butcher, dealer and chapman" - so had The Green Dragon again been used to sell beer?

According to the notice of auction in 1859 there was a brewhouse in the garden. Subsequent owners included the late Sidney Gordon Russell, afterwards Sir Gordon Russell, the furniture designer.

THE KING'S ARMS, High Street   19.

Parts of the building go back to the sixteenth century. The older part has mullioned windows on the first floor and a doorway with a triangular hood on attached Doric columns. The eighteenth-century part of The King's Arms has three storeys and three bays. There is a bow window on the ground floor and a doorway with fluted three-quarter columns. It was formerly called Ardley House. The Guild of Handicraft Trust has a recording of Mr Fred Coldicott telling the story of Miss Harwood, a well-to-do lady who lived there at the beginning of the century; she sent presents to Fred and his brothers, on one occasion giving Fred a Meccano set. In 1906 Dr John Dewhurst, the local doctor, lived at Ardley House and complained in a letter to *The Evesham Journal,*

The King's Arms

"Sir, Within the last few years, Campden has gradually wakened from its long sleep. For some considerable time we have had gas, both for lighting our streets and houses, as well as clean, dry pavements for walking upon, and now, quite recently, we have

45

obtained an excellent water supply.

"There remains however one relic of a barbarous past, which though picturesque, is an offence against the most elementary laws of sanitation and a source of annoyance to the nostrils of a large majority of the inhabitants of the town. I refer of course to the monthly sheep market, which is held in the very centre of the town, viz the Square. The penetrating odour left by the sheep is distinctly perceptible at the time I am writing this letter and that is more than 10 days since the last market.

"To those who have merely to pass by the place, the smell is offensive; to those who have unfortunately to live within a few feet of the saturated ground, is nothing short of disgusting. From personal experience I can state that in summertime the front rooms of my house are practically unfit for habitation, not only on market day, but for several days after.

"The nuisance is obvious, not only to those who have eyes to see, but to all who have noses of even average sensitiveness, and I trust the good sense of Campden will soon take steps to sweep away our monthly sheep market out of the Square."

The Sheep Market in the Square

The smell of the market became too much for the doctor and by 1913 he had moved to The Martins. Later Ardley House was owned by the

Cresswells, who moved to Charingworth Manor because of the smell of the sheep market and the flies that gathered around the sheep.

In 1935 it became The King's Arms. Miss Lloyd Roberts moved her tea room across the road from the old King's Arms pantry. The King's Arms is now a popular hotel, with comfortable restaurant and bars.

THE COTSWOLD HOUSE HOTEL, High Street   *20.*

This is a fine Regency ashlar-faced house with a portico with detached fluted Tuscan columns and a splendid curving staircase. The house was built in 1815 by Richard Miles, a prosperous merchant. He also remodelled North End terrace in Leysbourne, and Miles House there is named after him. He was elected bailiff several times and was obviously an important person in the town. He is buried in an altar tomb in a railed enclosure in the churchyard to the south of St James's church. He left a charity for the poor, which is referred to in the church, under the tower.

At the end of the nineteenth century Dr. Smith lived here, and his son the film actor Aubrey Smith was born here. Dr. Smith's assistant lived in Ardley house, now The King's Arms, and the cottages between the two buildings were used as the surgery. The blocked doorway which led to Ardley House can still be seen. These two cottages are older than the

The Cotswold House as a private house

47

house and it is possible they were on a packhorse lane that went through The Cotswold House grounds to the Noel Arms arch.

Mr Fred Coldicott in his book remembers Dr Morris living at Cotswold House. In 1918 Fred's brother Bill went to work for Colonel Paley there; he assisted in the garden, milked the Jersey cow and helped with the son's polo ponies. His wage was 8s. a week.

The last owners of The Cotswold House as a private house were Miss Warden and Mrs Wallace, who kept horses and dogs. Their Great Danes and Wolfhounds would bark behind the gates and the railings which then enclosed the front garden. Mrs Wallace and Miss Warden moved to The Paddock in Back Ends in 1938. Mrs Wallace was small in stature but she could be seen masterfully walking her huge dogs.

In 1939 Kelly's Directory lists Mr and Mrs James Hargreave as proprietors. From 1946 to 1954 Mr Daniels had the hotel and from 1954 to 1963 Vincent and Victoria Cotes were the proprietors. In 1963 Mr Graeme Black bought the hotel, and then Mr Black and Mr Geoffrey Douglass ran it. Some time in the mid-sixties Mr Black's brother looked after the hotel during one winter. When Mr Black returned from holiday his brother reported a peaceful watch, but asked, "Who was the rude woman who didn't speak when I said good morning?" On being questioned he described her dress. "That was Mrs Wallace," said Mr Black; her ghost had been seen by others before. In 1986 Mr Greenstock bought the hotel and a few years later it was bought by Mr and Mrs Forbes, who have given their name to the Forbes Bar.

Today The Cotswold House is a very elegant hotel and restaurant.

THE BEAR INN, Charlecote, High Street   21.

The Bear Inn is now part of the Cotswold House Hotel. It is an early eighteenth-century ashlar building, and has grouped windows with keystones and bull-nosed sills. The small building between The Cotswold House and Charlecote, now called Forbes, and also part of the hotel, contains a coaching arch which led through to the coach houses. To the left of the archway there had been a three-horse stable. There was a hayloft over the arch and this stable, with three openings for pushing hay down to each of three horses; when Mr Black took over the hotel he found hayseeds in the floor. There had been a round-headed opening to the courtyard at the back for loading hay in, which is now a plate-glass window. At the front the half-window over the arch is original; Mr Black added the round windows.

At the back of the Charlecote premises there was a cider-press with a lift for bottles. The first deed for The Bear Inn is a conveyance of 1730 from William White and Sarah his wife of Lechlade to Throckmorton Watts, a flaxdresser of Campden. According to Whitfield there was a flax mill in Campden up to at least 1838 which employed over 40 hands. In 1735 Throckmorton Watts mortgaged the property for £200 to Richard Horsman, fruiterer. It is still described as The Bear Inn. It would seem that Throckmorton Watts was unable to repay his mortgagee and was eventually forced to sell the property to him in 1744. It was still The Bear Inn, but that is the last time the name appears in the deeds.

The Horsmans (sometimes Horseman) seem to have been well established in Campden. Whitfield mentions a Samuel Horseman who was excluded from the panel at a visitation of heralds in 1682 on the grounds that although a burgess he was not a gentleman (perhaps because he was a Dissenter?) Sometime after 1738 Samuel and Richard Horsman leased the banqueting house and orchard next to the Coneygree. Probably Richard Horsman did not continue to use the house as an inn but as his private residence. It is mentioned in his will as "the messuage in my own occupation." He is still described as a fruiterer in his will, and was apparently a successful one. His son Edward, a mercer, inherited Charlecote, which was eventually to go full circle and become part of The Cotswold House Hotel.

A Campden Banknote from the 1790's

Edward and his brother John had been left a tidy fortune by their father, but they were led astray by over-ambition. They opened the Campden Bank in 1793 - one of the oldest in England outside London -

but sad to say it survived only four years before the bankruptcy commissioners wound up their estate and Charlecote was sold to meet the creditors. The house remained in private hands until 1915 when it was rented as a boarding house for girls at Chipping Campden school.

Before Mr Black's time the room left of the archway in what is now Forbes was the Gas Showroom, and the Gas Manager lived above. To the right of the passage two rooms were occupied by Mr Bower for his estate agent's business. He also lived here in the thirties. He was followed by Jackson, Stops & Staff.

Montrose, the house next to Charlecote, may also have been used as part of The Bear Inn at some stage. There is apparently some evidence of beer storage in the cellar of Montrose.

THE OLD HOUSE AT HOME,
now Green Dragon, High Street   22.

In 1867 Morris's Commercial Directory lists Thomas Savage, tailor and beer retailer, and the 1871 census shows him at The Old House At Home. In a book of drawings by F. L. Griggs, with an introduction by Russell Alexander, published posthumously in 1940, there is a drawing of the market hall and The Old House At Home dated 1918, and Alexander says "he [Griggs] had heard the elder Campden people talk with regret of the pulling down [closing down?] of an ancient inn, The Old House At Home."

THE GEORGE AND DRAGON,
now Dragon House, High Street   23.

The house has two dormer windows and a sundial. A central archway, once the doorway, is now a passageway to a house between two shops, at present the bookshop and a gift shop. There are wooden doors to an entry.

The George and Dragon had a long history as an inn. Its extensive stabling brought a great deal of market business to it, placed as it was so centrally. The earliest sale of the freehold, subject to a rent charge, seems to have been in 1619 by Basen and Jenks of the premises which became The George and Dragon. It was sold to Humphrey Painton, haberdasher, and was occupied by Cyprian James.

In 1816 it was kept by widow Mary Howe. The Campden Ratebook of 1821 shows William Wyatt as the owner occupier of what is called "The George Inn, & shop, buildings, garden etc. 1 rood 28 perches, value £12 10s, rates 6s 3d." In 1838 Pigot's Directory lists William Wyatt at what is still called The George. He is there in the 1841 census as "butcher and publican," and Slater's Directory in 1858 confirms that he was still there then. In 1879 the licence was transferred from John Jessop to Thomas Wood. The 1881 census shows Charles Kedward as innkeeper, with a lodger William Dunn, maltster's assistant.

The George and Dragon

In 1892 The George and Dragon, and the burgage[11] with its buildings on Back Ends belonged to William Wyatt's son William. In this year he sold the inn to Flowers Brewery in Stratford, with "Pig Sties, Trap House, Slaughter House, Stable, and Brew House," but retained the right of way for pedestrians, carriages with horses, carriages without horses, and the burgage with the cottages, where Wyatt's two sisters lived. At the turn of the century poor relief was given to somewhere called Wyatt's Yard, and Mrs Pamela Atkinson, who now lives in George and Dragon Cottage, thinks it is possible that this was the name of these cottages, and that they were very dilapidated. Later some of these cottages (there were nine very small ones in all) fell down or were condemned. Mr Fred Coldicott writes that in the thirties he had the unpleasant job as a boy of cleaning the privy in what was at that time called George and Dragon Yard.

The George and Dragon Yard

In 1946/47 the remaining five cottages were bought up and made into one, then called Campden Lawn but now known as George and Dragon Cottage, so preserving the name of the former inn at the other end of the burgage in the High Street.

Until 1854, when railway time came in, the town hall clock was regulated by a sundial on the wall of The George and Dragon. The sundial obviously gained much admiration: in *A Gem of the Cotswolds: Chipping Campden, Gloucestshire,* a book of photographs published in 1907, W.H.Taunt writes of Campden, "It is a charming old-world town, not yet spoiled with modern improvements, and in traversing it many artistic bits will be seen." One of these "artistic bits" was "a sundial over The George and Dragon." Mr Fred Coldicott remembers this as a pub until after the first world war. There was a way through to Back Ends; the door was closed once a year to keep control of the right of way. Mr Smith kept the pub. Delirium tremens led him to attempt suicide; he cut his wrists, was saved, and sadly sent to jail for three months.

In 1918 at the Campden Petty Sessions there was an appeal against closure. Richard Smith said that the customers were respectable; there had been no convictions and no transfer for five years; he had had seventeen men lodging there for hay baling, and the accommodation was good. The gross rental was £25.10s., net £20.16s. He pointed out that The Noel Arms and The Lygon Arms catered for a different class of customer. But the police said the footpath at the side of the inn made supervision difficult, and the inn lost its licence.

In the thirties there was a greengrocer's shop here, run first by the two Miss Potters and then by the Margetts.

Today besides the shops there is a pottery approached down the entry at the side.

THE GOLDEN COCKEREL, *now Westcote House, High Street* 24.

This is a house with a central gable and bay window next to The Seymour House Hotel. It has two dormer windows, mullioned and transomed windows and an oak door under a stone porch roof. The building dates from the seventeenth century; the deeds go back to 1652. In 1790 Richard Miles, grocer, of Campden bought the property (see The Cotswold House Hotel).

The Golden Cockerel

In 1926 Miss Baker bought the house. The family were hand loom weavers and traded under the name of The Kingsley Weavers, making mainly curtains and soft furnishings, probably in an upstairs room. The weaving business closed down in 1931. Mr H.L.Bennett, an old Campdonian, remembered "F.L.Griggs carried out some alterations in 1928. Miss Hargreave ... opened The Golden Cockerel about the beginning of 1932 and shortly afterwards leased Clifton House as an annexe to the hotel. She purchased Three Gables about 1953/54. She then had communicating doors put in joining the two properties. She gave up the lease of Clifton House when she bought Three Gables. When she retired she kept Three Gables for her own use and sold The Golden Cockerel to Mr Hugh Corbett of The King's Arms Hotel in 1969. After twenty months he sold The Golden Cockerel to Mrs Warren who, presumably not finding it a viable proposition, sold it in 1971 as a private house, when it reverted to its former name of Westcote House."

Mr Nevill New stayed at The Golden Cockerel during the fifties when he was on leave from the colonial service, " and very comfortable it was too."

Lord Kings Norton, the famous aeronautical engineer, lived here until his death in 1997.

THE SEYMOUR HOUSE HOTEL, High Street   25.

The building dates back at least to the early 1700s. It is a fine house with two storeys, seven grouped windows, a coved eaves cornice and a doorway with fluted Tuscan columns.

Between 1823 and 1855 Mr Turney lived in Seymour House. He is buried in the churchyard to the south-east of St James's church in an altar tomb on which is written, "In memory of James Turney who resided in this parish for 32 years during 14 of which he held the office of Parish Church Warden, in which as in all the relations of life he was highly

The Seymour House as a private house

esteemed for his upright and conscientious conduct."

In 1881 Fred Gimson, a retired marine mechanic and mariner, lived there with his wife and children; his elder brother John, a "merchant of Toronto," was also there when the census was taken.

At the turn of the century wealthy families from Birmingham spent their summers in Campden, arriving with their trunks and taking over large houses. Seymour House was one of these. The presence of these families could have been beneficial to the Guild of Handicraft as they could have provided a market for the work of the Guild.

In his book on Campden Mr Fred Coldicott remembers a Mr Welsh, who was nicknamed "Yabu". He was a huge man with a beard. He had a large sledge that the children used to borrow, and out at the back of the house he had a huge stuffed alligator brought back from his travels as an explorer.

At the beginning of the twentieth century there was a connection with Chipping Campden School: classes were held in Seymour House as well as The King's Arms and The Swan in 1915. In 1907 girls had been admitted to the school and in 1919 there was boarding for the girls at Seymour House. A large elegant room on the first floor was used as a dormitory, which rather obscured its elegance. The 1944 Education Act ended fee-paying and the boarding houses soon closed. Seymour House was auctioned at The Lygon Arms in 1946 by Alfred Bower. The grounds went back to Back Ends, with a stable block, wash-house, tennis court and an eighteenth-century summer house. It was bought by Norman and Helen Hitchman and initially they ran it as a guest house taking many persons displaced after the war - people who had lost their homes in the war or had been in the armed forces. Also several regular visitors came from Africa and India to work at Campden Research Station and learn the process of canning. Mrs Diana Harding, the daughter of Mr and Mrs Hitchman, remembers the Indian visitors bringing rice back with them. They would go into the kitchen and make curry for the family, which was much appreciated.

Meanwhile the buildings were restored and became a hotel in the 1950s. Many actors working in Stratford stayed in the hotel. The children of the actors and the two daughters of Mr and Mrs Hitchman would perform their own plays on a table in the garden, with a great deal of enthusiasm. The use of buildings follows changes in trade: as visitors increased the family moved first to the cottage converted from the stable and then in 1970 to what is now called The Malt House next door which they bought. Mr and Mrs Hitchman sold the hotel in 1987. A substantial part of the garden was subsequently sold for building, but the entrance gates in Back Ends still exist and gave their name to the small estate there, the Seymour Gate. The fine wrought iron gates were erected by Mr and Mrs Hitchman in the 1960s and have a preservation order on them.

The Seymour House is still a hotel and continues to adapt its buildings to changing conditions. The malthouse in the grounds, said to be the oldest malt barn in Chipping Campden, is now being converted into a conference centre, but it will retain many of its historic features. A painting on the first floor landing of the hotel shows the old conservatory at the back where teas were served until the 1980s; this is now a part of the dining room and the old grape vine still winds its way to the glass roof. It is a hotel and restaurant of great charm.

The Malt House was owned by James Turney along with Seymour House. His widow left the Malt House to her nephew Samuel Dunn in 1856. It stayed in the Dunn family until 1939. At the beginning of the twentieth century it belonged to the famous local character Dicky Dunn, who worked the maltings. He was not an industrious man, but preferred to spend his time looking out for the weather in the High Street and passing the time of day with his friends. A sign announcing "Richard Dunn, Licensed Maltster" appeared over his doorway in the High Street. (This blocked doorway can still be detected.) When his licence was not renewed, he simply crossed out "Licensed"; but occasionally he still made a little malt for a farmer.

Norman Jewson remembered the Dunns vividly. He would often stay there when in Campden. Martha Dunn, "a woman of forcible character, was the daughter of William Haines [from The Kettle] ... When she grew up she became a schoolmistress, travelling as far as the Hebrides to learn and so be able to teach hand-weaving and the spinning and dyeing of wool. Later on she came back to Campden where she married Dicky Dunn, a gentle and submissive little man with very little to say for himself in the presence of his masterful wife, although her sharp tongue had a kind heart behind it ..." Martha Dunn was one of the few local people who welcomed the newly arrived Guildsmen in her house. She would mend their socks and generally mother them. Later she kept a shop in her house.

A seventeenth century ashlar building with mullioned leaded windows and two dormers, this house occupies a pleasant site next to Pinkney's House opposite Church Street. "Mow" is a stack, and "Barley Mow", a stack of barley, was a simple indication that beer was sold. One commentator on pub signs tried to suggest it came from "bel amour", the French for sweetheart, but the former explanation seems by far the more likely, if more prosaic. Rushen states that for thirty or forty years this was kept by Alf Stanley and that a close of one acre at the rear was formerly known as "Pinkey". In the deeds this was also sometimes "Pinkie" and then "Pinkney". Rushen adds that it had not been a beerhouse "for more than some forty years" (since about 1870). The census of 1881 shows it not, indeed, as a pub, but lived in by Henry G.Ellis, his son, their wives, and two male lodgers; the four men were all basket makers. Henry Ellis employed four men and one boy, and they made baskets at what is now the greengrocer's in the High Street. The baskets were made from osiers which grew down by the Cam, and would have been in great demand, as everything - fruit, meat, bread, - was carried in baskets. Some baskets, used as a measure, were known locally as "pots;" plums, apples, potatoes, beans and peas were all sold by the "pot" in Evesham market. Henry Ellis also sold fish, and in the Whit Monday processions of 1895 he appeared on a decorated cart as Neptune with four sea nymphs.

In 1936 The Ancient Buildings Trust of Lincoln's Inn Fields sold The Barley Mow, "a messuage, formerly a beerhouse" to Mrs Edith Hart, wife of George Henry Hart of Ivy House.

Today it is still a private house.

THE OLD EIGHT BELLS,
now The Convent, and Leasebourne House, Leysbourne 27.

At the top end of the town, just before the corner of Back Ends, these houses form an interesting group of buildings. The Convent has two dormer windows and a stone porch roof over the door and stone dog tooth brackets along the eaves. Leasebourne House (next door to the Convent) has three storeys, a coved eaves cornice and a magnificent porch with Tuscan columns. It is described in the earliest deed of 1634 as Pretty's House, having been formerly occupied by John Pretty. It is consistently referred to as Pretty's from 1640 to 1708 and there is no mention in the deeds of The Old Eight Bells until the property is joined to the present convent next door. In 1708, 1793, 1809 and 1835 the two properties together are described as formerly or "anciently" The Old Eight Bells. They were joined and separated and joined again. In 1793 Thomas Smith sold the properties to Richard Lumbert, surgeon and apothecary. The deeds refer to a "messuage, formerly called or known by the name or sign of The Old Eight Bells." Between 1809 and 1869 the deeds refer to The Old Eight Bells and in 1874 there is the last reference to it. In 1874 James Horn bought both properties from Mrs Rutherford. There was some doubt, however, as to the identity of the two properties. This was apparently resolved by a declaration made by John Herbert Kingzett, aged 82. "The dwelling house lately occupied by Mrs Seitz (a tenant in the Convent) being ... the premises ... formerly The Old Eight Bells or some part thereof or standing and being on the site thereof or of some parts thereof." This must have cleared things up nicely. It would seem, however, that The Old Eight Bells was on the site of what is now St. Paul's Convent. It may have been a medieval hostelry.

Mr H. Griffiths writing in 1947 says of The Old Eight Bells that it was "the bell-ringers' pub in former days.... The way to St James's church in those days was through the tithe-yard from Leysbourne; and the entrance to the belfrey was through the two stone pillars, incorporated in the churchyard wall to the left of the present steps (and still there). When the approach to the south doorway of the church was altered - probably when the original lime avenue was planted in 1770 - the stone masons altering the then wall, incorporated in it the two old pillars, like milestones, thinking it such a pity to do away with them. The lime avenue - six each side in honour of the Twelve Apostles - having been planted in the eighteenth century brings The Old Eight Bells Inn - with its short cut to the church tower - to a date well before 1770." While this is not an entirely coherent argument, it does preserve a story attached to The Old Eight Bells, and is not inconsistent with the evidence from the deeds. Incidentally he adds: "Later on, when the limes were old enough to blossom, people would gather the flowers to brew lime-juice tea. This made a cooling drink for summer."

THE RED LION, now Wold Cottage, Broad Campden   28.

This is an attractive old thatched cottage at right angles to the lane. J.

P. Nelson says that Wold Cottage was once The Red Lion Inn. It was later the Post Office and also a shop. In the 1920s Granny James kept the shop and the Post Office. Unfortunately the deeds were burned at some stage and no information from them exists. C. R. Ashbee rebuilt Lion Cottages next door.

THE BAKER'S ARMS, Broad Campden 29.

The Baker's Arms is a seventeenth century building. Its sign includes three sheaves of wheat and a hand weighing them on a balance, a reminder that on the Day of Judgement souls would be weighed too, and anyone who had given short measure would be punished. So the sign is a statement of the honesty of this particular baker who will be happy to be judged. It was so named because it was once a bakery, the actual bakehouse being thought to have been on the right of the car park. Inside there are exposed stone walls, dark beams, on a dark brown ceiling - possibly the traces of many pipes of tobacco - and fireplaces at each end of the bar, where part of the floor is tiled to cater for country footwear.

In 1871 Thomas Keyte was baker and beerhouse keeper here, showing yet again how landlords would have other trades. In 1917 the pub was run by the Bricknells, who had previously been at The Angel. Old Mr Bricknell was a wheelwright and a blacksmith. *The Evesham Journal* of 26 January 1918 records that on 14 December 1917 Mr Bricknell had been informed that his son, Pte H. Bricknell, was missing. They had now heard that he was a Prisoner of War in Germany. He had been 21 months in the trenches, then home for five months in hospital, and returned to France in 1917. He had joined up with his brother at the outbreak of war; the brother was killed on the Somme in 1916.

Mr and Mrs Nobes took over the Baker's Arms from the Bricknells. Many local characters such as Jimmy Teapot with the large appetite (and so called

Jimmy "Teapot" Williams

because he was always eating and drinking) and Charlie Ladbrook the postman frequented this inn. According to J.P.Nelson in his book on Broad Campden there used to be a picture by Lionel Edwards in the bar of The Baker's showing Charlie Ladbrook on his pony joining in the hunt after his round was over, his letter-bag flapping from his back. H. J. Massingham wrote in 1931 with great appreciation of The Baker's Arms and its customers. "... Behind the counter Mrs Nobes ... clicked her needles and smiled on the company beamily, her golden hair done up in a tight bun that caught the light and splintered it. There too was Jimmy Teapot, and the talk was of his breakfast, which had consisted of two sheep's-heads, a rabbit whole, 'one peck of spuds and vower onions'. He called for half a dozen raw eggs, which he cracked on the lid of his scrumpy mug and poured into the pale liquid. He ... emptied it at one swoop ... then summoned his usual quartern loaf and block of Cheddar and settled down to have 'summat to yut.'" Such were pub lunches in those days.

Some people (including the novelist Graham Greene when he lived in Campden in the thirties) have taken a sceptical view of this story, on the grounds that eggs were expensive (twopence each in winter) and that Jimmy Teapot would not have been able to afford so many. But this is not conclusive.

The Baker's Arms has pleasant rural views.

THE ANGEL, Broad Campden 30.

The building no longer exists. The Angel Inn gave its name to Angel Lane. The Ordnance Survey Map of 1900 shows The Angel Inn as the first building on the left down the lane to the side of St Michael's church. There used to be a way to the back of The Angel from the end of Meeting House Lane, where the Quaker Meeting House is. In 1841 George Whitford was publican. In 1858 Slater's Directory lists John Such as landlord; in 1867 Morris's Commercial Directory mentions him as landlord and wheelwright, and in 1881 a John Such was still there. After that it was kept by the Bricknells; J.P.Nelson writes, "Big Bill Bricknell was known as Tadpole, because he was all head with a small body." He was also a wheelwright. The Angel was then kept by Matthew Williams, also a rag and bone merchant, and finally by Mrs Byrd and her sons. It was owned by Joseph Whitford of Bretforton.

The Angel was one of six pubs closed down in 1918. At the Petty

Sessions, Superintendent Hopkins said Broad Campden was a small hamlet of Campden. There were two licences, The Angel and The Baker's Arms. The Angel was 120 yards from the road but there was a footpath by it. The customers were of the labouring class. The licence was transferred to Mrs Byrd, a widow, by her son who had lost his life on active service. The gross rental of The Angel was £18.10s., net £14.16s.8d. Mrs Byrd said this was the only full licence in Broad

The Angel

Campden and she had been frequently called out in the night to supply brandy and spirits in cases of illness. Their average takings were about 13s. a day. Mr Barker, who was representing the owner and licensee, said the house had been in the Whitford family for over a hundred years, and pressed for a renewal of the licence. It was not granted, however, and the case was referred to the Compensation Authority. The Byrds moved to Corner Cottage, where they sold mineral waters.

The Buntens were the last to live in the building after it was an inn. Mr Fred Coldicott says, "When the building was demolished, stone from The Angel was used to build the priest's house behind the Roman Catholic church in Chipping Campden" - this would have been in 1935.

Unlocated Inns

There are intriguing references to several inns which cannot so far be placed accurately on the map.

In 1593 a deed in the Earl of Northampton's archive relates to "*an Inne* and Leys Close adjoining Little Close leased by Walter Nicolls for twenty shillings of lawful money of England for one year."

61

Alice Gold, widow, was landlady of *The King's Head,* where in 1712 and 1715 evidence was taken concerning a suit brought by the vicar over the payment of tithes. (Jewson and Griggs called the old King's Arms The King's Head, but it is not clear why.)

Most fascinating of all, an 1810 deed of St Anne's in the High Street refers to premises "formerly a public house known by the name or sign of *The Mermaid,*" occupied by Mary Stanley, with an acre of pasture behind, being sold to Thomas Herbert by the Earl of Northampton. It is puzzling that a Cotswold town should have a Mermaid. Interestingly enough, in 1706 there were also two Mermaids in Burford. Perhaps the name was not an attempt to attract the seafaring trade, but a tribute to the London tavern where Shakespeare (more or less a local lad) drank. Shakespeare did after all retain Cotswold connections, even if they were somewhat tenuous (Thomas Russell Esq., who owned the manor of Broad Campden, was the overseer of Shakespeare's will); and this was the period of a romantic revival of interest in Shakespeare and things Shakespearean.

The Tariff Inn is said to have been in Cutts Yard, but no evidence has been found for this.

The Old Thatched Tavern was listed by The Cotswold Chronicle of 6 February 1968 as one inn "known to have existed in Chipping Campden of yore," but no dates are known.

According to Whitfield a seventeenth-century lease refers to an inn in Campden called *The Holy Lamb.* Rushen speaks of a house known as The Lamb House, on the same side of the street as the grammar school, "probably where Mrs Clarke's shop is now" (1911). The deeds of The Plough and The Elm mention The Lamb. The earliest documents are a lease and release dated 9 and 10 January 1728. The owners were then Thomas Smith Esq. of Tenbury and George Gardner Esq. of Evesham, and they sold the house to William Freeman of Campden, mason, for £31. 10s. Thomas Woodward, also a mason, was a party, apparently as Trustee.

The Lamb House has not been certainly identified but Mr Peter Gordon thinks it was possibly what is now Keeley's Cottage next to The Plough. The last reference to the Lamb House is 1839, 30 years before the first date in Keeley Cottage deeds. The Lamb House was then "lately" in the occupation of a John Smith. In 1869 a John Smith acquired Keeley Cottage. Was this a family connection? And was the Lamb House the site of that evocatively named inn, The Holy Lamb?

A Fictitious Inn

In his thesis on Chipping Campden, Dr Craig Fees describes an occasion in 1934 when the BBC made a regional "Microphone at Large" programme about Campden, which purported to be set in an inn but was actually recorded in a private house. The atmosphere of an inn was captured very successfully: local people talked about farming and thatching, building and making cider. There was an extract from a Mummers' Play, and Morris Dancing with music, bells and clapping. The star turn was to be Polly Waine, aged 94 and the oldest inhabitant. But on the night Polly simply refused to appear, put her light out in her almshouse and went to bed. She later said, "Maybe if they had called for me a bit earlier I might have thought more of it." During the course of the programme the microphone at large was forgotten, and people behaved naturally, as of course they were intended to. But the BBC got more spontaneity than they bargained for when at one point someone shouted, "You shut thee bloody mouth." "Bloody" was an unspeakable word at the time, and the BBC received many letters of complaint. It was said in a national newspaper that Campden had put the B into the BBC.

No one in Campden, however, would reveal who uttered the offending word. Campden people knew how to live and let live.

Pigs in Campden High Street outside The Live and Let Live

63

NOTES

[1] C. R. Ashbee came from a wealthy London family. At Cambridge he was influenced by the works of Ruskin and William Morris, and in 1888 he was instrumental in setting up a Guild of Handicraft in Whitechapel, to establish a better way of working and living for craftsmen. In 1902 the Guild moved from the East End of London to Campden so that the Guildsmen could be closer to nature and live the "simple life." He set up workshops in the old silk mill in Sheep Street, where some of the crafts continued to be practised.

[2] F. L. Griggs trained as an architect but worked as an artist and illustrator and became famous for his etchings of topographical scenes. He was preparing drawings for Macmillans's *Highways and Byways* series when he first came to Campden. He was so charmed by the town that he decided to stay. He lodged at Braithwaite House, 1904-5, leased Dover's House until 1927, then designed Dover's Court in Back Ends for himself. He became a Catholic in 1912; in 1935 he designed a new priest's house next to the Roman Catholic church. He helped greatly to conserve the town between the wars.

[3] The Noel family: see under The Noel Arms.

[4] Norman Jewson, whose book *By Chance I Did Rove* describes his first visit to Campden in 1907, was a young architect who came from London following the Arts and Crafts trail to the Cotswolds. He spent much time in the area. He was a close friend of F. L. Griggs, working with him on various projects and restoring buildings in the town.

[5] Dover's Hill games, or Dover's Meeting. Robert Dover started the "Cotswold Olimpicks" in 1612. Held on the Thursday and Friday of Whitsun week, they included races, sports and games on Dover's Hill above the town. The games ceased in the Civil War, but revived with the Restoration and continued without a break for the next two hundred years. In 1852 they were stopped as the drinking and rioting accompanying them had got out of hand, but in 1951 they were brought back to life as part of the Festival of Britain, and by 1966 they were once again a regular feature, as they are today.

[6] i.e. a match

[7] Now Calf Lane.

[8] A road or lane along which cattle were driven.

[9] George Henry Hart was a silversmith with the Guild of Handicraft when it moved to Chipping Campden in 1902. From 1912 he took on the running of the workshop, joined in 1930 by his son Henry Hart. This tradition is now carried on by his grandson David Hart along with Derek Elliot, and William and Julian Hart.

[10] Defoe, in *A Tour Through the Whole Island of Great Britain (1724-6)*, explains a statute: "A meeting of servants for hire, which the people there call a Mop; 'tis generally in other places vulgarly called a statute, because founded upon a statute law in Queen Elizabeth's time for the regulating of servants."

[11] In the Middle Ages plots of land or burgages were granted to the burgesses of Campden by the lord of the manor, to whom they paid a rent. The burgages stretch behind the houses on both sides of the High Street.

BIBLIOGRAPHY

Peter Clark, *The English Alehouse. A Social History 1200-1830*
    (Longmans, 1983).
Leslie Dunkling and Gordon Wright, *The Wordsworth Dictionary of Pub
    Names* (Wordsworth Editions, 1994).
David Verey, *Gloucestershire: the Cotswolds,* ed. Nikolaus Pevsner
    (Penguin, 1979).

W. H. Taunt, *A Gem of the Cotswolds: Chipping Campden,
    Gloucestershire* (1907).
David Viner, *North Cotswolds in Old Photographs* (Allan Sutton, 1988.)
Views of Campden (W.Horne, n.d. [before 1910]).

P.C.Rushen, *The History and Antiquities of Chipping Campden* (2nd
    edition, privately published, 1911).
J. G., *Chipping Campden Today and Yesterday* (T.Elsley, High Street
    Campden, 1931.)
Christopher Whitfield, *A History of Chipping Campden* (Shakespeare
    Head Press, 1958).
Geoffrey Powell, *The Book of Campden* (Baron, 1967).
J.P.Nelson, *Broad Campden* (Privately published, 1971).
J.P.Nelson, *Chipping Campden* (Privately published, 1975).
Catherine Gordon, *Towns and Villages of England: Chipping Campden*
    (Allan Sutton, 1993).
F.W.Coldicott, ed. Craig Fees, *Memories of an Old Campdonian*
    (CADHAS, 1994).

Rev. F. E. Witts, *The Diary of a Cotswold Parson, selected by David
    Verey* (Allan Sutton, 1978).
H.J.Massingham, *Wold Without End* (Cobden-Sanderson Ltd., 1932).
H.J.Massingham, *Shepherds's Country* (Chapman and Hall Ltd., 1938).
Norman Jewson, *By Chance I Did Rove* (privately published, 1973).
Mary Elizabeth Lucy, *Mistress of Charlecote. Memoirs of Mary
    Elizabeth Lucy*, introduced by Alice Fairfax-Lucy (Gollancz,
    1987).

Index of Persons

Dybble, Harold 14
Edwards, Lionel 60
Elliot, Derek 66
Ellis, Henry G. 57
Elsley, Thomas 14, 24, 25
Fairweather, Joe 24
Fairweather, Mrs   24
Fees, Craig 19, 63
Forbes, Mr & Mrs 48
Freeman, George 10, 11
Freeman, William 62
Gardner, George 62
Garfield, John 20
Garfield, Thomas 20
Gibson, James 34
Gimson, Fred 55
Gimson, John 55
Gladwin, Millicent 11
Gold, Alice 62
Gordon, Peter 62
Greene, Graham 60
Greenstock, Mr 48
Griffin, Richard 41, 42
Griffiths, Miss 40
Griffiths, H. 14, 35, 58
Griggs, F. L. 6, 18, 25, 37, 50,
        53, 62
Gurton, Mark 30, 31
Haines, James 9
Hall, Richard 44
Hand, Richard 20
Hands, Sarah 10
Harding, Diana 55
Hargreave, James 48
Hargreave, Miss 53
Hargreave, Mrs 48
Harris, Bernard 42
Harris, John 6, 24
Harris, Mr & Mrs Tom 11

Harrison, Lewis 20
Harrowby, Earl of 14
Hart, David 66
Hart, Edith 57
Hart, George Henry 35, 57
Hart, George 35
Hart, Henry 66
Hart, Julian 66
Hart, Maj. William 14
Hart, William 66
Hartwell, John 39
Harwood, Miss 45
Harwood 25
Hawley, Michael 21
Haydon, J. 39
Herbert, Thomas 62
Hewins, Nancy 32
Hicks, Sir Baptist 29
Hicks, Lady Juliana 29
Hitchman, John 16
Hitchman, Helen 55, 56
Hitchman, Norman 55, 56
Holloways 32
Holton, James 34
Hopkins, Supt. 61
Horn, James 58
Horne 16
Horsman, Edward 49
Horsman, John 49
Horsman, Richard 49
Horsman, Samuel 49
Howe, Mary 50
Howley, Michael 39
Howley, Thomas 39
Hudson, Capt. 32
Hughes, John 28
Ireson, George 10
Izod, William 16
James, Ciprian 50

James, Cyril 38
James, Mrs 59
Jeffrey, Annie 4, 17
Jeffrey, William 17
Jenks 50
Jenks, John 36
Jessop, John 51
Jewson, Norman 9, 12, 27, 38, 62
Jones, John 17
Jones, Muriel Tudor 10
Jones, Supt. 39
Kedward, Charles 51
Keen, John 24, 39
Kennedy, Frank & Jane 10
Keyt, John 20
Keyte, Thomas 59
Kings Norton, Lord 54
Kingzett, John 15
Kingzett, John Herbert 58
Knight, Lodge 34
Ladbrook, Charlie 13, 35, 39, 60
Ladbrook, Edwin 11
Ladbrook, Lawrence 35
Lane, John 2, 23, 24
Lane, William 21
Lardner, Henry 42
Lloyd, Fr. 32
Lumbert, Richard 58
Lygon, General E. P. 16, 17
Malin, Thomas 42
Manton, George 34
Margetts 53
McRae, Supt. 39
Meadows, Joe 14
Merriman, Thomas 21
Miles, Robert 15, 16
Miles, Richard 47, 53
Miller, Alec 6
Monk, Supt. 20

Moss, Thomas 8
Morris, Dr 48
Moule, C. L. 35
Moule, Keith 35
Mullins 16, 17
Mullins, Hugh 29
Nailor, John 44
Neidpath, Lord 7
New, Nevill 9, 11, 21, 22, 24, 54
Nicolls, Walter 61
Nobes, Mr & Mrs 59, 60
Noel, Hon. C. N. 29
Noel, Edward 29
Noel, Sir Gerard 15
Noel, Rev. H 38
Noel, Robert 43
Northampton, Charles Earl of 43
Northampton, Marquess of 44
Osborne, James 21
Osiris Players 3, 32
Owen, Katherine 43
Painton, Humphrey 50
Paley, Col. 48
Palmer, Sarah 20
Payne, Alexander 23
Pennycock, Alex 7
Perry, James 16
Phipps, Frederick 39
Potter, Leonard 14, 15, 18
Potter, Molly 11, 12
Potter, the Misses 53
Pretty, John 57
Rathbone, Mr 42
Richards, Mrs 34
Rimell, John 31, 39
Roberts, Miss Lloyd 47
Russell, Sir Gordon 45
Russell, Thomas 20, 62
Rutherford, Mrs 58

Sadler, James 11, 13
Sadler, Sam 11
Sadler, Mrs 13
Sambrook, Samuel 17
Savage, Thomas 50
Sellers, William 10
Sharp, B. 39
Sheldon, William 28
Shervington, Job 21
Sinclair, Hilary 43
Sinclair, Paul 43
Skey, John 4, 17, 18, 21
Skey, Mrs 18, 21
Slatter, John Robert 21
Smith, Aubrey 47
Smith, Rev. Elisha 29
Smith, John 63
Smith, Nathan 44
Smith, Richard 52
Smith, Thomas 16, 62
Smith, William 34
Smith, Dr 47
Stanley, Alf 57
Stanley, John 15, 16, 63
Stanley, Joseph 16
Stanley, Mary 62
Stanley, Peter 10
Starkiss, Mrs 37, 38
Stead, Richard 21
Stewart, Seumas 38
Such, John 60
Tanner, Albert 31, 32
Taplin, Alfred 21
Taylor, Robert 33
Taylor, Tommy 18
Timms, Fred 39
Timms, James 20
Toft, Hanna 26
Toft, William 25, 26

Tomes, Emanuel 41
Tomes, Mr & Mrs John 6
Tomes, Mr 34
Turner, Ray 42
Turney, James 17, 29, 44, 54, 56
Turney, Mary Ann 17, 44
Usher, Thomas 34
Waine, John 39
Waine, Polly 8, 63
Wakeman, Charlie 32
Walford family 34
Wallace, Mrs 48
Walters, W. 16
Warden, Miss 48
Warmington, Allan 8, 30, 40
Warmington, Joe 25
Warmington, W. H. 31
Watts, Throckmorton 49
Welch, Robert 36
Welsh, "Yabu" 55
Whatcote, Stephen 36, 37
Whatcote, Elizabeth 37
Wheatley, Samuel 44
White, Sarah 49
White, Thomas 16
White, William 49
Whitfield, Christopher 25, 32
Whitford, George 60
Whitford, Joseph 60
Williams, Jimmy "Teapot" 59, 60
Williams, Matthew 60
Wilson, Bob 35
Wilson, Jean 35
Wilson, John 27
Wood, Thomas 51
Woodward, Edward 36
Woodward, Thomas 62
Wyatt, John 30, 44
Wyatt, William 51

Financial Assistance for this
publication is gratefully
acknowledged from the
following breweries:

BASS MITCHELLS AND BUTLERS

SCOTTISH COURAGE

WHITBREAD BEER COMPANY (FLOWERS)

HOOK NORTON BREWERY CO. LTD.

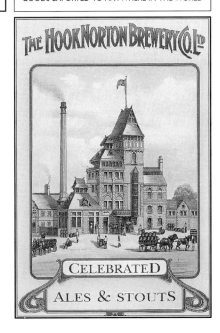